Walking Eye App

EXP

MARR

●●●○○

INSIGH
Walk

▦ SCAN QR C

◎ DESTINAT

⛭ SHIPS

📖 EBOOKS

🌐 TRAVEL BL

✈ ACTIVITIE

⚙ SETTINGS

ⓘ ABOUT

HOW THE DESTINATION CONTENT WORKS

Each destination includes a short introduction, an A–Z of practical information and recommended points of interest, split into 4 different categories:

- Highlights
- Accommodation
- Eating out
- What to do

You can view the location of every point of interest and save it by adding it to your Favourites. In the 'Around Me' section you can view all the points of interest within 5km.

HOW THE EBOOKS WORK

The eBooks are provided in EPUB file format. Please note that you will need an eBook reader installed on your device to open the file. Many devices come with this as standard, but you may still need to install one manually from Google Play.

The eBook content is identical to the content in the printed guide.

HOW TO DOWNLOAD THE WALKING EYE APP

1. Download the Walking Eye App from the App Store or Google Play.
2. Open the app and select the scanning function from the main menu.
3. Scan the QR code on this page – you will then be asked a security question to verify ownership of the book.
4. Once this has been verified, you will see your eBook and destination content in the purchased ebook and destination sections, where you will be able to download them.

Other destination apps and eBooks are available for purchase separately or are free with the purchase of the Insight Guide book.

CONTENTS

MARRAKECH OVERVIEW   6

IN THE MOOD FOR...   8

NEIGHBOURHOODS   26

  Central Medina   31

  Southern Medina   57

  Northern Medina   81

  Guéliz   105

  Hivernage, Menara, Palmeraie, Environs   125

  Marrakech Region   143

ESSENTIALS   162

INDEX   172

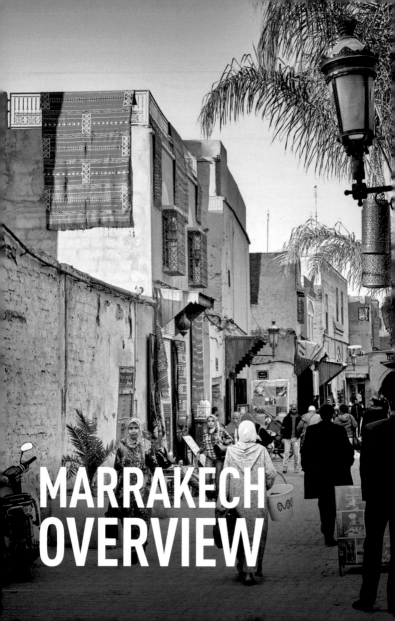

MARRAKECH
OVERVIEW

Marrakech is arguably the most exotic, mysterious, and enchanting city this close to Europe. The 'Red City', capital of the Great South, was once a place of such importance that it gave its name to Morocco. Its thousand-year history is rich and turbulent, with an eclectic cast of characters: sultans and nomads, magicians and slave-traders, fortune-hunters and colonialists. Now it attracts movie stars, writers, and artists – and tourists looking for something a bit different.

In the 1960s and '70s, Marrakech lured hippies, playboys, rich expats, and the fashion elite. It was one of the coolest and also the most artistically inspiring places to escape to and, often, reinvent yourself in. Today, Marrakech is experiencing its latest renaissance as a city looking to the future. Quirky new boutiques are springing up alongside the medina's colourful ancient souks; an array of restaurants, concept stores, bars, cafés, and thriving modern art galleries have reached Guéliz (the new town); tranquil villa retreats and some of the best boutique and five-star hotels in the world have set up shop; and a wealth of adventures can be had on its doorstep – from skiing to hot-air ballooning, camel-trekking and horse-riding. This desert city at the crossroads of cultures has reinvented itself yet again as a hip, romantic, adventurous getaway for those who want a little spice in their holiday.

Marrakech is undoubtedly not for everyone. This is a city with edge. It is contradictory and not easily fathomed, but for most people who visit, that is all part of its elusive charm. From the exotic market stalls of the medina to the westernised glamour of Guéliz, Marrakech is a riot of contradictions and extremes – at once African and Arab, eastern and western, desert town and modern city, religious and secular, elegant and rough-round-the-edges. At times daunting, occasionally maddening, always exhilarating, Marrakech is all about getting lost, letting go, and opening up to whatever experience or encounter comes your way.

IN THE MOOD FOR...

...SOUKS, BOUTIQUES, AND MARKETS

From the souks filled with exotic treasures and stalls of spices piled high to fabulously chic boutiques selling everything from kaftans to kids' clothes, you could be forgiven for thinking that Marrakech is all about the shopping. For many it is, and exploring the magical labyrinthine **souks** (see page 40) should be first on your list of things to do in the city. Watch master craftsmen at work and haggle for lanterns, carpets, soft leather slippers *(babouches)*, and Berber jewellery.

For foodies, the colourful **Mellah Market** (see page 67) in the old Jewish quarter is an essential stop, where you will find seasonal fruit and veg, flowers, preserved lemons and olives, and butchers' stalls. There is also the **Spice Square** (see page 39), lined with apothecaries brimming with thousands of spices, potions, cosmetics, and even chameleons. If you're in the market for a carpet, the **Criée Berbère** (see page 52)

is the place to go and if it's serious gold jewellery, head to the dazzling **Grande Bijouterie** (see page 78).

Vintage-lovers won't be disappointed either. Not only are the main souks dotted with antique stores selling everything from Leicas to 1950s Coca Cola signs, but the northern medina has one of the best flea markets south of Paris. **Souk el Khemis** (see page 95) is a little-known goldmine where you will find Victorian gramophones, 19th-century oil paintings, 1960s furniture, and painted doors from ancient riads. Fittingly, for a city like Marrakech, there are some genuine **Aladdin's caves** (see page 94) in the medina, where movie producers and celebrities are known to shop.

If you are craving a western hit where things come with price tags, there are dozens of new **boutiques in the medina** (Souk Cherifia, see page 47 and Rue Riad Zitoun el Jdid, see page 75), several high-end antique places on **Rue Dar el Bacha** (see page 93), and a wealth of shops in **Guéliz** (see page 108), where you can find Western takes on kaftans, stylish homewares, and contemporary design, and even Moroccan haute couture.

... STREET FOOD

Western restaurants with price tags to match appear all over Marrakech and it's sometimes easy to forget that you are in Morocco, not Paris or London. There is no more vivid reminder of where you are, and no more authentic or unusual eating experience to be had, than through Marrakech's street food. Underrated and often wrongly viewed with apprehension, street food is an exotic taste-fest and a window onto a different world.

The soul of Marrakech street food is found at the **food stalls of Jemaa el Fna** (see page 37), where you can eat anything from snails to grilled sheep's head, and from spicy *merguez* sausages to succulent chicken *brochettes* for just a few dirhams. There are stalls and makeshift restaurants all over the city, for this is how most Moroccans eat when they are not at home, but **Méchoui Alley** (see page 54) and long-standing institution, **Chez Bejgueni**, in Guéliz (see page 123) should not be missed.

... A SPECTACLE

The whole city of Marrakech is a spectacle and just walking through the medina can throw up a kaleidoscope of experiences. But the soul of the city's theatrical life is the square of **Jemaa el Fna** (see page 34), where a thrilling thousand-year-old nightly show (some call it the greatest on earth) unfolds like a magic carpet at sunset. There are acrobats and magicians, storytellers and snake charmers, and all manner of spontaneous entertainment in between.

Its name means either 'Assembly of the Dead' or 'Mosque at the End of the World.' The great trans-Saharan caravans, laden with spices and slaves, salt and gold, once arrived here.

Today, by day, it is the preserve of Gnaoua musicians, dentists, witch doctors, juice sellers, and dancing monkeys. This is also the place to visit a fortune-teller – an ancient practice still thriving in a country where concepts of superstition and *baraka* (luck) are threaded through society.

... PAMPERING

Souks, spectacles, and fine dining aside, you could also come to Marrakech just for the spas. The art of the hammam (or steam bath) is ancient, dating back millennia, and is an essential part of both religious and social life in the Arab world. Cleanliness is one of the basic tenets of Islam – water is considered sacred – and the hammam is as much a part of daily life in Morocco as the mosque. This is where people come to socialise with friends, catch up on neighbourhood gossip, discuss business and even arrange marriages.

In Marrakech, virtually every hotel these days has a spa or hammam, so for many you won't even need to leave your hotel to get pampered. Visiting a traditional, local hammam, such as the **Hammam Dar el Bacha** (see page 101), where you will be flung into the heart of communal life and scrubbed to within an inch of your life,

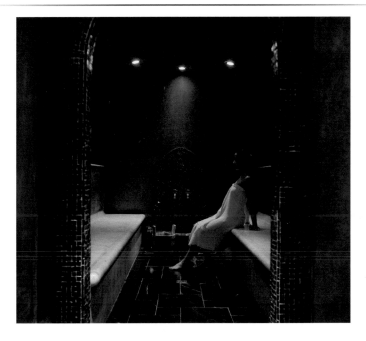

may not be everyone's idea of heaven, but it's an authentic Moroccan experience and will illuminate a side of Marrakchi life usually hidden from tourists.

For those who want a more refined spa, without losing the charm of a traditional hammam, there are two in the medina: **Les Bains de Marrakech** (see page 66) and **Hammam de la Rose** (see page 101).

But for the very pinnacle of pampering and uber-luxe indulgence, book into the exclusive spas of five-star hotels, such as the **Royal Mansour**, **Ksar Char-Bagh**, the **Four Seasons**, and the **Clarins Spa** at the **Royal Palm Marrakech** (see page 133), where the best in modern cosmetics and spa treatments are combined with unimaginably opulent surroundings.

... ENCHANTED EVENINGS

A candlelit table strewn with roses in the courtyard of a 500-year-old palace, the starry African night above, course after course of exotically flavoured dishes... Dinner in a riad in Marrakech is a wonderfully romantic experience.

The best in the medina are **Dar Yacout**, where movie stars and royalty like to eat, **Dar Zellij**, set in an opulent original 17th-century courtyard (see page 92), and **Pepe Nero**, which is housed in the former palace of Pasha Glaoui (see page 49).

One of the most acclaimed restaurants in Marrakech is run entirely by women: **Le Tobsil**, where the set menu changes every day and is sourced from local markets (see page 49). **Le Fondouk** (see page 98) is located in a beautifully restored old artisanal riad, where Marrakech's vibrant history as a trading city permeates the atmosphere. For post-dinner glamour, there is belly dancing at **Le Comptoir** and live music at the opulent **Jad Mahal** (see page 128).

... DECADENT DAYS

As Mae West once said, 'too much of a good thing can be wonderful!' Plunge pools on rooftops, luxurious villas nestled in palm groves, cool courtyard gardens... For lazily decadent days, Marrakech has it all.

Several glorious riad hotels in the medina are open to non-residents. Give yourself some down time at **Les Jardins de la Koutoubia**, **Riad el Fenn** or **Les Jardins de la Medina** (see page 48), or the **Royal Mansour** (see page 133), all of which have stunning pools, delicious food, and sumptuous spas.

In the elegant suburb of Hivernage, five-star hotels such as the **Four Seasons** (see page 132), offer day passes for the use of their pools and lunch for non-guests. Outside town, head to poolside oases such as Les Deux Tours in the Palmeraie or Beldi Country Club, which is a five-minute drive from the medina (see page 130).

For the ultimate treat, have afternoon tea or cocktails at **La Mamounia** (see page 72); or, for something a little more amped-up, the pool at **Nikki Beach** is a people-watching paradise (see page 130).

... SULTANS AND SPLENDOUR

Marrakech is saturated with history: it seeps through the city's streets and the stonework of the buildings – the palaces, riads, and ruins are wreathed with ghosts of the past. It is easy to imagine great Saharan caravans entering the gates of the city; picture sultans holding court in glittering palaces and battles raging outside the medina walls.

The most obvious testament to Marrakech's past is the **Koutoubia Mosque and Minaret** (see page 36), the spiritual heart of the city. This is a magnificent monument to the 12th-century Almohad era, when Marrakech flourished as an intellectual and cultural centre.

The rosy mud-brick **ramparts** (see page 38) that encircle the medina hold the key to much of Marrakech's history: every gate (or *bab*) has meaning, every battlement tells a story. Morocco has long been famed for its exquisite art, architecture, and craftsmanship, as illustrated by these gates and other buildings – from stucco carved like lace and finely painted cedar-wood doorways to jewel-like *zellige* tile-

work and delicately soaring arches and columns.

Nowhere is the splendour of Marrakech better visualised than in the atmospheric ruins of the 16th-century **Badi Palace** (see page 76), which were once adorned with marble and gold, and in the spectacular courtyards of the **Bahia Palace** (see page 64), where sultans held sway.

The glittering **Saadian Tombs** (see page 68) are a fitting resting place for the kings of Morocco. Head for the **Musée de Marrakech** (see page 88) and the **Musée de Mouassine** (see page 45) to learn about the city's history amid splendid collections of arts and crafts.

The **Madrassa Ben Youssef** (see page 84) is one of the most tranquil and architecturally inspiring buildings in the city, while the remarkable **Koubba** (see page 103), the oldest building in Marrakech, evokes bygone worlds. Finally, the **Chrob ou Chouf** fountain (see page 102), dating from the 16th century, is a fitting example of the importance of water here on the edge of the desert.

... A GLAMOROUS NIGHT OUT

Nights in Marrakech can sparkle with glitz and glamour if that is what you're after. You can have rooftop cocktails with a view at the **Bab Hotel**, the **Sky Lounge at The Pearl Marrakech**, or at the **Renaissance Hotel's Sky Bar** (see page 113), or you can listen to funky live music at **Kechmara**, **African Chic** (see page 117), and **Jad Mahal** (see page 128).

The hip crowd hangs out at **Bo et Zin** and **Le Comptoir**, while die-hard clubbers head to **Theatro** and **Suite Club** (see page 128).

... FAMILY FUN

The sensory experiences of **Jemaa el Fna** and the **souks** (see pages 34 and 37) cannot fail to spark little imaginations, but there's a wealth of activities beyond the medina that the whole family will love.

For young thrill-seekers, **Terres d'Amanar** offers activities including horse riding, mountain biking, zip-lining, and treetop adventures (see page 141). If you'd prefer a unique desert experience, go **camel trekking** in the Palmeraie (see page 140) or camping in the **Agafay Desert** (see page 156).

There is yet more fun to be had at vast **Oasiria water park**; **Casa Botanica**, which has a kids' play area, rabbits and a charming café (see page 140); and sculpture-filled **Anima Garden** (see page 152).

... SOME PEACE AND QUIET

Marrakech can be hectic, hot, and dusty, but it also has peaceful sanctuaries where you can get away from it all. The Red City is famous for its luxuriant gardens. Yves Saint Laurent's **Jardin Majorelle** (see page 108) is one of the most iconic in the world and a magical spot to spend an afternoon. In the centre of buzzing Guéliz, there are two peaceful gardens: **Jnane el Harti**, with lofty palms and ancient olive trees, and the **Cyber Parc**, an 8-hectare (20-acre) 18th-century royal garden (see page 121). The **Agdal Gardens** (see page 70) were created for the sultan's pleasure and are full of picnicking Marrakchis today. There is nowhere more atmospheric than the **Menara Gardens and Pavilion** (see page 129) at sunset, with its backdrop of snow-capped Atlas Mountains. But even in the thick of things and in the most unlikely places are hidden refuges. In the medina, there are **rooftop restaurants** far above the madding crowds (see page 34), as well as magical **Le Jardin Secret** (see page 55). The **Jewish cemetery** (see page 71) and **European cemetery** (see page 115) are unusual yet quietly beautiful places of reflection.

... SPORTING ADVENTURE

If your dream holiday is an active one, Marrakech is well equipped with places where you can keep fit and engage in a variety of sports. Many of the facilities are first-class and enthusiasts can enjoy one of the best climates in the world, with year-round sunshine, very little rain, and warm temperatures that only become uncomfortably hot in the months of July and August.

Marrakech has positioned itself as one of the world's premier golfing destinations (the king is a keen golfer). Many of the courses (see page 136) are exotically landscaped and dramatically situated, with amazing views of the High Atlas. Fit for a king and Winston Churchill, the **Royal Golf de Marrakech** is the oldest course in Morocco and still one of the best. Designed by Robert Trent Jones, the **Palmeraie Palace**

is a firm favourite and the **Amelkis Golf Resort** and **Samanah Country Club** both offer challenging golf on stunning courses.

If it's tennis you prefer, the **Royal Tennis Club**, **Atlas Tennis Marrakech Academy**, and the **Four Seasons** (see page 132) all offer good courts and lessons in beautifully-kept grounds. There are several companies that offer camel safaris, horse-riding (see page 140), and **quadbiking day trips** (see page 158), with miles of exhilarating trails to explore, or even **white-water rafting** in the Ourika Valley (see page 150). For a more laid-back adventure, you can soar over the city in a **hot-air balloon** (see page 139) or check in to a yoga retreat (see page 135).

For those who want a truly quirky experience, a **bicycle or vintage-sidecar ride** through the alleyways of the medina is one of the best ways to see the old city (see page 87).

... CULINARY DISCOVERY

Marrakech is a food-lover's paradise, and with influences from Africa, the Middle East and France, food is definitely one of the highlights of a visit here.

Explore a dazzling array of local ingredients in the bustling **Mellah Market** (see page 67) and the charismatic **Spice Square** (see page 39). Then put your skills to the test at the cookery schools of **La Maison Arabe** or **House of Fusion**, where classes include a trip to the market (see page 90). But it's not all tagine and couscous: Guéliz is crammed with alternatives, from **Asian restaurants** such as **Katsura** (see page 120), to French bistros **Le Studio** and **Kechmara**, where the expat crowd likes to eat (see page 112).

... TRADITIONAL CRAFTS AND CONTEMPORARY DESIGN

Artists have been drawn to Morocco for centuries, but in the 21st century it is home-grown Moroccan artists and contemporary designers that are inspiring aesthetically inclined visitors. If you think Marrakech is all about the past, think again.

In the medina there are several unique 'art houses', such as **Ministero del Gusto** (see page 42), that showcase quirky design and the work of local artists. The **Dar Si Said Museum** (see page 74) has one of the best exhibitions of Moroccan arts and crafts in the world, while **Maison Tiskiwin** (see page 79) takes you on myriad journeys through the collection of a veteran anthropologist and explorer. The beautiful photographs at **Maison de la Photographie** (see page 89) reveal a Morocco that once was; in contrast, at the cutting edge of the contemporary Moroccan art scene are dozens of eye-opening contemporary **art galleries** and a crop of new **concept stores** in Guéliz (see pages 110 and 108). For die-hard design lovers, a little-known secret is the industrial area of **Sidi Ghanem**, which is jam-packed with design, lighting, and furniture shops, as well as a couple of funky restaurants (see page 134).

... ESCAPING THE CITY

Taking a day trip or two outside Marrakech can give a real taste of Morocco as a whole. Whether you choose to explore mountain, rural, or coastal Morocco – all of which are within surprisingly easy reach of Marrakech – you will encounter famously hospitable people, revel in some of the most glorious landscapes on earth, and have an experience that you will remember forever.

The **High Atlas Mountains** (see page 146) are just an hour from Marrakech, and the region around Mount Toubkal and the village of Imlil offers a wealth of hiking and trekking possibilities in a magnificent part of Morocco that has changed little in centuries. The foothills of the Atlas are also studded with restaurants with arresting views and charming places to spend the day or base yourself for an Atlas trek – try opulent **Kasbah Bab Ourika** or **La Roseraie** (see page 148).

The fertile **Ourika Valley** (see page 150) is a rural utopia, with eco-museums, hotels, and aromatic gardens to discover – all less than an hour from the city.

To really cool down – and to enjoy some spectacular scenery – head for the seven waterfalls of **Setti Fatma** (see page 153) or the dramatic **Cascades d'Ouzoud** (see page 159).

Adrenalin junkies are spoilt for choice, from **helicopter rides** over the Atlas and into the Sahara for lunch (see page 155) to **skiing on the highest piste in Africa** in the little resort of **Oukaimeden** (see page 149). The stunning **Agafay Desert**, just 40 minutes from Marrakech, has two exceptional

luxury camps: La Pause and Scar-abeo Camp, where you can sleep under the stars or just escape for a desert lunch (see page 156). And then there's **Lalla-Takerkoust**, a stunning lake at the foot of the High Atlas ringed with excellent restaurants, many offering water-skiing and wake boarding (see page 154).

For the ultimate day trip, have lunch by the sea in enchanting **Essaouira** (see page 160). This windswept town has everything: characterful white-washed build-ings, fresh seafood, a vast crescent of golden beach where the wind-surfing, surfing, and kite-surfing is first-class, and a sleepy medina full of antique shops and art galleries.

NEIGHBOURHOODS

Marrakech is divided into the medina (the old town) and Guéliz (the Ville Nouvelle or new town). To help you get around, we've divided the medina into central, northern, and southern neighbourhoods. Guéliz is a separate neighbourhood; Hivernage, the Menara, Palmeraie, and environs are covered in a separate chapter, and excursions in the Marrakech region are highlighted in the final section.

Central Medina. This is the geographical heart, spiritual soul, and tourist hub of the medina. Everything in this area – demarcated at its southern end by the gardens of the Koutoubia and at its northern edge by Rue Dar el Bacha – revolves like a whirlpool around the iconic Jemaa el Fna with its age-old nightly spectacle. The souks stretch north of the square, and the magnificent Koutoubia Mosque at the neighbourhood's western edge stands sentinel over the whole of Marrakech.

Southern Medina. The grandest part of the medina, this southern neighbourhood has a colourful cultural history and is where you'll find many of the city's most chic riads. Made up predominantly of the original fortified kasbah, the royal palace, and the *Mellah* (Jewish quarter) with its colourful markets, the area is punctuated by the great imperial palaces of Marrakech (the Badi and Bahia palaces, and the Saadian Tombs), some wonderful museums celebrating the city's heritage, the legendary Mamounia hotel, and the Agdal Gardens, where Marrakchis picnic in summer.

Northern Medina. Far from the bustle of the souks, the northern triangle of the medina is, for the most part, refreshingly undiscovered. Traditional, tranquil residential life is played out around the tomb of Marrakech's most revered patron saint, Sidi Bel Abbes; vintage-lovers can spend hours exploring the rambling flea market of Souk el Khemis; south, closer to the souks, are galleries, *fondouks*, boutique shops, romantic riad restaurants, tailor's shops, and hammams, the Musée de Marrakech, and the atmospheric Madrassa Ben Youssef.

Guéliz. Often undeservedly overlooked, super-relaxed Guéliz has some of the best and most varied restaurants in town – from sushi and Thai to Lebanese, Italian, and French. Its leafy side streets are dotted with charming shops where everything has a price tag and there is no need to haggle; fantastic modern art galleries showcasing Moroccan and international artists; outdoor cafés that are great for people watching; and Yves Saint Laurent's Jardin Majorelle, a breath-taking sanctuary in the heart of the city.

Hivernage, Menara, Palmeraie, Environs. Hivernage, the wealthy residential district, is all about private houses and large chain hotels, but it also has some of the best nightclubs and hippest bars in town. On the edge of Marrakech is the mesmerising Menara Pavilion and to the north is the fabled Palmeraie, home to some of the most luxurious villas, spas, and exclusive hotels in Morocco. Nearby, there are tennis and golf clubs, while the more adventurous can head off on camel safaris, horse-riding and quad-biking adventures, or take a hot-air balloon ride.

Marrakech Region. Within three hours of Marrakech there is a wide range of excursions to take. From lunching beside the serene waters of Lake Lalla-Takerkoust to surfing the crashing breakers of Essaouira on the Atlantic coast; from skiing in the morning to white-water rafting in the afternoon; and from the high-adrenalin thrill of a helicopter ride to the relaxed vibe of a country restaurant with a panoramic view, the region of Marrakech exemplifies the diversity of Morocco in dazzling microcosm.

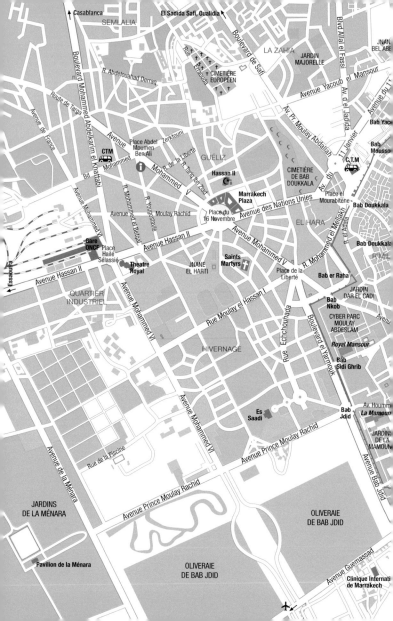

CENTRAL MEDINA

Watch one of the world's greatest shows unfold at Jemaa el Fna 34

Soak up the atmosphere at sunset when the *muezzin* calls 36

Test your tastebuds at Marrakech's legendary food stalls 37

Ride around the medina walls in a horse-drawn carriage 38

Treat your senses to the exuberance of the Spice Square 39

Explore Marrakech's fabled souks, an artisanal treasure trove 40

Drop by three unique 'art houses' for cutting-edge art and design inspiration 42

Patronise the hippest boutique shops in the medina 43

Shop with a conscience at a women's cooperative 44

Wonder at the craftsmanship of two historic riads 45

Lunch on a roof terrace overlooking the medina 46

Discover Souk Cherifia – a contemporary boutique collective 47

Have a sunlit lunch and then cool off in a chic pool 48

Feast like a sultan at one of Marrakech's best Moroccan restaurants 49

Forget haggling and shop for arts and crafts at the price-set Ensemble Artisanal 50

Splurge on an unforgettable evening at the magical Royal Mansour 51

Take home a one-of-a-kind Moroccan carpet 52

Eat a mouth-watering Marrakchi speciality... slow roast lamb 54

Discover a secret garden in the heart of the medina 55

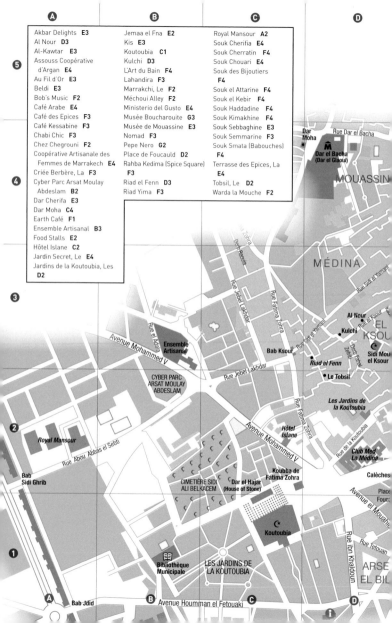

Akbar Delights **E3**
Al Nour **D3**
Al-Kawtar **E3**
Assouss Coopérative
  d'Argan **E4**
Au Fil d'Or **E3**
Beldi **E3**
Bob's Music **F2**
Café Arabe **E4**
Café des Epices **F3**
Café Kessabine **F3**
Chabi Chic **F3**
Chez Chegrouni **F2**
Coopérative Artisanale des
  Femmes de Marrakech **E4**
Criée Berbère, La **F3**
Cyber Parc Arsat Moulay
  Abdeslam **B2**
Dar Cherifa **E3**
Dar Moha **C4**
Earth Café **F1**
Ensemble Artisanal **B3**
Food Stalls **E2**
Hôtel Islane **C2**
Jardin Secret, Le **E4**
Jardins de la Koutoubia, Les
  D2

Jemaa el Fna **E2**
Kis **E3**
Koutoubia **C1**
Kulchi **D3**
L'Art du Bain **F4**
Lahandira **F3**
Marrakchi, Le **F2**
Méchoui Alley **F2**
Ministerio del Gusto **E4**
Musée Boucharouite **G3**
Musée de Mouassine **E3**
Nomad **F3**
Pepe Nero **G2**
Place de Foucauld **D2**
Rahba Kedima (Spice Square)
  F3
Riad el Fenn **D3**
Riad Yima **F3**

Royal Mansour **A2**
Souk Cherifia **E4**
Souk Cherratin **F4**
Souk Chouari **E4**
Souk des Bijoutiers
  F4
Souk el Attarine **F4**
Souk el Kebir **F4**
Souk Haddadine **F4**
Souk Kimakhine **F4**
Souk Sebbaghine **E3**
Souk Semmarine **F3**
Souk Smata (Babouches)
  F4
Terrasse des Epices, La
  E4
Tobsil, Le **D2**
Warda la Mouche **F2**

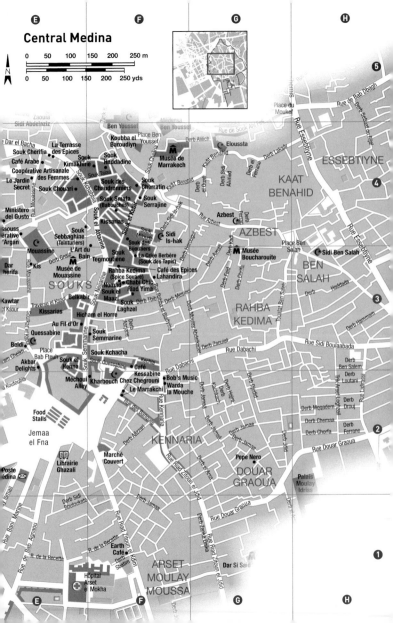

Watch one of the world's greatest shows unfold at Jemaa el Fna

Jemaa el Fna, the iconic physical and cultural heart of Marrakech, is a primal, ancient, intangible space that has been referred to as, 'an inland, tideless sea'. Gathering place for a thousand years, this is where the great Saharan caravans, laden with spices, slaves, and salt would arrive from Timbuktu. Today, the goods may have changed, but not the sense that here Africa and Arabia converge. At once circus, open-air food festival, and living museum, it is the distillation of Marrakech's mystique and magic.

At first glance, Jemaa el Fna is uninspiring. But spend a few hours here and the essence of

this place will slowly reveal itself. During the day, it is the preserve of orange-juice vendors, nut and dried fruit stalls, vibrantly attired water-sellers, henna tattooists (be sure to use the red henna – the black contains chemicals), dentists with displays of human teeth, herbalists selling powdered bones and ostrich eggs, Gnaoua musicians with their noisy castanet-like *qraqabs*, and fortune tellers – a pre-Islamic practice still deeply engrained in Moroccan life.

But when the *muezzin* calls and the sun sinks, everything changes. Now, Jemaa el Fna's famous **food stalls** (see page 37) materialise and the fragrant smoke from a hundred *grillades* wafts into the night air. Beneath the glow of a single bulb, families laugh and eat, while around them the music of the Gnaoua mingles with the dying cries of the *muezzin*, the shouts of competing food vendors and the excited buzz of hundreds of people soaking up the atmosphere.

In the shadows are dozens of ever-expanding and decreasing circles of men. In the centre, you may see a magician vanishing something into thin air, a snake-charmer playing his flute, or – if you are lucky – a wizened man in a cloak telling a tale in classical Arabic with an egg and a length of rope as illustrative props. These are the famed *halqias* (storytellers), whose stories have been passed down through the centuries. They are a dying breed, but remain the soul of Jemaa el Fna and the reason why the area was declared one of Unesco's first Masterpieces of the Oral and Intangible Heritage of Humanity. It is the people that make Jemaa el Fna what it is, filling the space with its unique energy.

Experiencing Jemaa el Fna is all about diving into the madness. But if it gets a bit much, take sanctuary in one of the restaurants that line the square. **Chez Chegrouni** is an old favourite with a fantastic view from the roof terrace and excellent Moroccan food with vegetarian options. **Café Kessabine** has equal views and fine food, while **Le Marrakchi** has more expensive food (and belly-dancers) and is the only place on the square that serves alcohol – tempting for a cocktail at sunset.

Chez Chegrouni; Jemaa el Fna; tel: 0665 47 46 15; B, L, D; map F2
Café Kessabine; 77 Souk Kessabine, Jemaa el Fna; tel: 0635 82 98 26; B, L, D; map F3
Le Marrakchi; 52 Rue des Banques, Jemaa el Fna; tel: 0524 44 33 77; B, L, D; map F2

Soak up the atmosphere at sunset when the *muezzin* calls

When the sun sets, the haunting sound of the *muezzin* calling out the evening prayer fills the air. The *isha'a* – the last of the five daily prayers, (one of the Pillars of Islam) – is particularly magical.

In Marrakech, the **Koutoubia Mosque** (Mosque of the Booksellers – so named because it was once surrounded by booksellers; map C1) is the first to lead the call – with hundreds of others following in an echo that washes over the city. Unusually, all the calls to prayer here are 'live'; in most other Islamic countries they are recorded. Built in the 12th century by the Almohad caliph, Yacoub el Mansour, the minaret is the tallest structure in Marrakech at nearly 70 metres (230ft) and exactly five times as high as it is wide. A masterpiece of design, it was the model for the Tour Hassan in Rabat and the Giralda in Seville. Although the mosque is closed to non-Muslims, the *minbar*, from which the imam would lead the prayers, can be seen in the Badi Palace (see page 76).

The best place to soak up the atmosphere is from the tranquil **Koutoubia Gardens**, which afford a wonderful close-up view of the minaret glowing against the indigo sky, or from the roof of the **Hôtel Islane** opposite.

Hôtel Islane; 279 Avenue Mohammed V; tel: 0524 440 081; www.islane-hotel.com; map C2

Four globes

Traditionally, every minaret is surmounted by three globes at the very top of the tower, but the Koutoubia has four. Legend has it that these globes were once made of gold and that the fourth globe was forged out of the melted-down jewellery of Yacoub el Mansour's wife as her penance for breaking one day of the Ramadan fast.

Test your tastebuds at Marrakech's legendary food stalls

Marrakech's **food stalls**, on Jemaa el Fna (map E2), are arguably the most famous in the world. For this reason, they may seem like just another tourist trap, but this is one of the few places where an average Marrakchi family will eat out.

Eating here is an experience not to be missed and one that you will never forget. For those who are prepared to sample the unusual and quirky delights of the stalls, there is an art to this open-air extravaganza. Word of mouth is key. If someone in-the-know has recommended a particular stall, eat there. Failing that, go to the ones that are full of locals. An empty stall on a busy night is not a good sign. Don't be put off by vendors waving menus in your face and herding you towards their stall as they wax lyrical in a dozen languages. Retain your sense of humour. Don't be afraid to try something new.

Mustafa No. 1's snails are famously good and the grilled **sheep's head** is surprisingly tasty. For the less adventurous, **merguez sausages**, *kefta* (spicy meatballs), hearty *harira* soup (lentil, chick pea and tomato), *b'stilla* (chicken or pigeon with almonds in flaky cinnamon-dusted pastry), and succulent **chicken brochettes** are classic Moroccan street food favourites.

Some stalls also have deliciously simple **grilled fish**, served with a wedge of lemon, a pile of chips or *khobz* (bread), and spicy green chili on the side. Sit wherever there is space, shout your order at the chef and tuck in. Eating is done with your hands (always use your right), drinks are soft, and the whole thing – along with the crazy theatrical spectacular that is Jemaa el Fna – will set you back just a few dirhams. Foodie heaven.

Ride around the medina walls in a horse-drawn carriage

Marrakech's *calèches* – horse-drawn carriages – are as much a part of the city as the mosques and motorbikes. For something a little bit different and a lot more atmospheric, take a ride in the evening when the walls are dramatically lit by the setting sun.

The main *calèche* stand is on Place du Foucauld (map D2) next to Jemaa el Fna. The **Tour des Ramparts** takes in all 16km (10 miles) of Marrakech's medina walls. The oldest parts date to the foundation of Marrakech in the 12th century and were built by Almoravid sultan Ali Ben Youssef to protect the city from Almohad attack. The walls – 10 metres (33ft) high, 2 metres (6.5ft) thick and built out of pisé (rammed earth) – are punctuated by 18 gates, or *babs*. **Bab el Khemis** (Thursday Gate) marks the entrance to Marrakech's fantastic flea market (see page 95), **Bab Dbagh** (Gate of the Tanners) leads to the pungent tanneries, **Bab Ghmat** was breached by Almohad mercenaries in 1147 as they laid siege to the city; **Bab Agnaou** (Black Gate) – a soaring horseshoe arch with intricate carvings framed by inscriptions of the Qur'an – is the most magnificent of them all and the entrance to the royal kasbah, and **Bab Ahmar** (Red Gate) was built by the Almohads exclusively to be used by sultans to gain entry to their palaces.

The carriages fit four people and you should agree the price before you set off. It should be no more than 120dh for the whole carriage for an hour.

Treat your senses to the exuberance of the Spice Square

The Rahba Kedima or **Spice Square** (map F3) bursts with magic. Nowhere is the fusion of Africa and Arabia that so characterises Marrakech more apparent than in this vibrant, ancient square.

Visit the apothecaries, where you will find live chameleons, turtles, lizards, leopard and zebra skins, roots, barks, herbs, leaves, seeds, horns, tusks – cures for everything, from arthritis to a broken heart – as well as herbal remedies, cosmetics, and toiletries: cochineal powder for rouge, kohl, henna, natural crystal deodorant, herbal 'Viagra', toothbrush twigs, and essential oils of amber, musk, rose, patchouli, and orange blossom.

For foodies, there is a plethora of spices: saffron (ask for the good stuff under the counter), argan oil, cumin and coriander, mace, star anis, cinnamon, and home-made spice mixes such as ras el-hanout.

In the middle of the square are piles of handmade baskets, wooden *harira* spoons, hats, and fresh produce from the countryside. The old slave market, now **La Criée Berbère** and the best place to buy carpets (see page 52), is through an alley off the north side. There are also two great restaurants here: **Café des Epices**, which has fresh juices, salads, sandwiches, and free Wi-fi, and **Nomad**, a retro, super stylish restaurant with a roof terrace, eclectic modern Moroccan food, and fantastic cocktails. Don't miss **Chabi Chic** on the ground floor (see page 43).

Café des Epices; 75 Rahba Kedima; tel: 0524 391 770; B, L; map F3
Nomad & Chabi Chic; 1 Derb Aarjan, just off Rahba Kedima; tel: 0524 38 16 09; B, L, D; map F3

Explore Marrakech's fabled souks, an artisanal treasure trove

The souks of Marrakech are the largest in Morocco and famed throughout the world as one of the most exotic places in the world to shop. They are also the oldest part of a city that thrived on commerce – and still does.

Historically, all souks were divided and laid out according to separate commodities being made and sold, with the most valuable products (gold, manuscripts) positioned in the centre of the main souk area and lesser goods radiating out from there. Today, little has changed. Each souk is still named after the product being sold and, aside from allowances for modern tastes, the goods are much as they would have been a thousand years ago.

The souks thread north from Jemaa el Fna and continue in a winding labyrinth until they hit the **Musée de Marrakech** (see page 88). Open from around 9am to 9pm, the best time to visit is in the cool of morning, or in the evening when the sun seeps through slatted roof shades, illuminating a million golden dust motes.

The main artery of the souks is **Souk Semmarine** (map F3), a broad, covered alley that begins with pottery and ceramics (look out for the much sought-after green Tame-groute pottery) and pâtisserie and moves into good quality fabric and textiles shops, selling everything from kaftans to pashminas, and huge, expensive, tourist emporiums full of antiques, carpets, and jewellery. About halfway along, Souk Semmarine forks. On the right is the **Spice Square** (see page 39) and on the left is **Souk el Attarine** (map F4), gleaming with copper and brass lanterns, mirrors, candlesticks, silver teapots, and lamps, as well as spices and perfumes (for which it was traditionally known).

Souk Smata (map F4) is unmistakably the shoe souk, with brightly-coloured and sequined *babouches* (Moroccan slippers). Leading off Attarine is **Souk el Kebir** and **Souk Cherratin** (both map F4), the preserve of leatherworkers and the place to go to buy bags, belts, wallets, and purses. To the left of Souk

Tips for haggling

Don't ask the price of something unless you are willing to start negotiating. Be prepared to take your time. The general rule of thumb is to offer half of the seller's first price and go from there. There is never a 'correct price' – if you want something and are happy to pay the price, then you have paid the right amount.

el Kebir are the *kissarias*, selling clothing and fabrics. There are some great little shops here, too, with chic lanterns, glassware, baskets, and antiques. To the right of Kebir is the jewellery souk, **Souk des Bijoutiers** (map F4). Nowhere is Morocco's living craftsmanship better illuminated than in the working carpenters' and blacksmiths' souks – **Souk Chouari** (map E4) and **Souk Haddadine** (map F4), at the northern edge of the

souks. These fragrant, noisy alleys are refreshingly un-touristy. To the southwest of this main cluster of streets is **Souk Sebbaghine** or **Souk des Teinturiers** (map E4) – the dyers souk, where rich iridescent skeins of wool and silk coloured with indigo, saffron, mint, poppy, and rose blaze against the sky. Music lovers should explore **Souk Kimakhine** (map F4), where traditional Moroccan and Gnaoua instruments are sold.

Drop by three unique 'art houses' for cutting-edge art and design inspiration

You won't know what's hit you when you step inside the mad world that is **Ministero del Gusto**. Established in 1998 by Fabrizio Bizarri, a designer, and Alessandra Lippini, former fashion editor of Italian Vogue, Ministero del Gusto is a homage to their passion for the beautiful and the unusual in everything from Italy to Africa, Pop Art to Art Deco, furniture to high fashion.

The tribal sculptures and rough ochre walls of the courtyard are pure Africa; the leather bath fed with water from a tree and the one-off pieces of furniture are sheer fantasy; the eclectic art pieces on the walls are windows onto every conceivable world; and Alessandra's vintage clothing and jewellery collection will send fashionistas straight to heaven.

Hassan Hajjaj – 'Morocco's Andy Warhol' – spent three years creating **Riad Yima**, his home-cum-Pop Art gallery: a temple to Moroccan kitsch. Come here to see his acclaimed photographs of Marrakech life and quirky 'upcycled' design, much of which is available to buy in the shop. There is a small café on the roof terrace.

Le 18 is also well worth a visit, established by photographer Laila Hida as a creative platform and exhibition space promoting artistic and cultural exchange. The riad supports local artists through residency programmes and exhibitions. There is also a literary café and events are held on a semi-regular basis.

Serious arty types may want to plan their trip to coincide with the **Marrakech Biennale**, a major contemporary arts festival promoting cultural dialogue and diversity, held every two years (see www.marrakechbiennale.org).

Ministero del Gusto; 22 Derb Azzouz, Mouassine; tel: 0524 42 64 55; by appointment only; map E4
Riad Yima; 52 Derb Aarjan, Rahba Kedima; tel: 0524 39 19 87; map F3
Le 18; 18 Derb el Ferrane, Riad Larouss; tel: 0524 38 98 64; map page 82 D2

Patronise the hippest boutique shops in the medina

Fashionable boutiques are springing up all over the medina. It's not just about the souks these days.

Akbar Delights (Place Bab Fteuh; map E3) is so successful that it now has shops in Paris and Rome, as well as at La Mamounia (see page 72). There are hand-embroidered kaftans and bejewelled slippers, beaded bags, Indian silk cushions, and sculptures from West Africa. **Beldi** (9–11 Rue Mouassine; map E3) began as a tailor's in the 1940s and is *the* place to go for haute couture: chic kaftans, velvet coats, vintage fabrics, and jewellery.

Kulchi (1 Rue el Ksour; map D3) has a great collection of rugs, carpets, and homewares (appointment only). Visit **Au Fil d'Or** (10 Souk Semmarine; map E3) for snakeskin *babouches*, cashmere cloaks, and fine cotton kaftans. **Kis Boutique** (36 Rue Mouassine; map E3) is a little gem, selling contemporary Moroccan clothing and accessories. If you've been to a hammam, you'll want to take home some of Morocco's *savon noir* (black soap). **L'Art du Bain** (Souk el Badine; map F4) produces fragrant 100% natural handmade soaps. The boutique at **Riad el Fenn** (see page 48; Derb Moulay Abdullah Ben Hezzian;

map D3) stocks vintage clothes, accessories, and jewellery, as well as art books, perfume, and fine bed linen. **Chabi Chic**, beneath Nomad restaurant (see page 39; map F3), sells stunning Moroccan-inspired table and kitchen wares with a modern twist.

Don't miss more boutiques in the Northern Medina (see page 93), Guéliz (see page 110), and Sidi Ghanem (see page 134).

Shop with a conscience at a women's cooperative

In a country where most textiles are handmade by women, it pays in more ways than one to shop at a cooperative, where all profits go directly back to the artisans, enabling them to support their families.

The **Coopérative Artisanale des Femmes de Marrakech** (67 Souk Kchabbia; map E4) sells beautiful hand-stitched cotton and linen clothing and home accessories, and will make items to order. Buy genuine cosmetic and culinary argan oil from the **Assouss Coopérative d'Argan** (94 Rue Mouassine; map E4). **Al Nour** (57 Rue el Ksour; map D3) is a professional training centre for disabled women who create natural fibre, hand-embroidered bed and bath linen, and simple tunics, dresses and shirts for men, women and children. **Al-Kawtar** (Derb Zaouia, numero 3; map page 82 B1) also employs disabled women who fashion embroidered linens, kaftans, and dresses. This concept has even spread into the restaurant scene, with the opening of the popular **Amal Centre** in Guéliz (see page 116) and the **Henna Café** (93 Arset Aouzal; map page 82 C2), which serves food, gives henna-painting classes, and stages art exhibitions – with all profits going towards an education centre for local Moroccans.

Check out online artisan-led marketplace **Anou** (www.theanou.com) for carpets, furniture, and jewellery made by master craftsmen that ship worldwide straight from the artisan's village in the Ait Bougmez valley. Maryam Montague of **Peacock Pavilions** (see page 135) has established an inspiring charity, **Project Soar**, which works with more than 250 Moroccan girls from rural communities to provide after-school support and activities. Visit their website (www.projectsoarmarrakesh.org) to see how you can help.

Wonder at the craftsmanship of two historic riads

Fifteenth-century **Dar Cherifa** is one of the oldest and most prestigious riads in the medina. Its restoration was undertaken using traditional materials and techniques and employing master craftsmen, ensuring complete authenticity. Its simple grandeur – carved stucco and filigree woodwork, soaring whitewashed arches and delicate *zellige* tiling – is breath-taking. The history of the house and Morocco's cultural heritage now live on through regular art exhibitions, literary salons, cooking, calligraphy and ceramics workshops, and musical evenings. Lunch is available on the roof terrace (on request, between noon and 4pm).

Nearby, Patrick Manac'h, of Maison de la Photographie (see page 89), discovered a hidden gem of a riad, now the **Musée de Mouassine**, which illuminates the beauty of 16th-century domestic Saadian architecture and gives a taste of a typical nobleman's house of the time. Under a layer of plaster, Manac'h uncovered pink gypsum walls, carved, delicately-coloured stucco pillars, and painted wooden ceilings, which were sensitively restored using skilled artisans. What were once the hammam and stables have been transformed into

a museum housing antique Berber carpets and traditional decorative arts. The museum also hosts regular art and photography exhibitions, documentary screenings, and musical evenings.

Dar Cherifa; 8 Derb Chorfa Lakbir; tel: 0524 42 64 63; daily 9am–7pm; map E3
Musée de Mouassine; Derb el Hamma, Rue de Mouassine; tel: 0524 38 57 21; daily 9.30am–7pm; map E3

Lunch on a roof terrace overlooking the medina

After a morning spent battling through the souks, what better way to take a breather than by retreating to a breezy roof terrace for lunch?

One of the few places in the medina that has an alcohol license, **Café Arabe** is on the edge of the main souks. You can either sit under old orange trees in the blue courtyard or on the roof terrace, with incredible views over the medina, the Koutoubia, and the High Atlas mountains. With an Italian/Moroccan menu that includes lasagne, tagine, and *briouates* (stuffed pastries), this is one of the best places for lunch in the medina, with reasonable prices – around 300dh for two.

Kamal Laftimi's (of Le Jardin, see page 51) **La Terrasse des Epices** is round the corner and, though it doesn't serve alcohol, it has better food and a funky terrace. Giant woven lanterns hang like globes above you and low tables are surrounded by comfy seating for tired bodies. The food is delicious – the succulent chicken and beef *brochettes*, light lamb, date and almond tagines, crème brûlée, and spiced canelle oranges will make you want to come back again for dinner. Expect to pay the same as Café Arabe.

Café Arabe; 184 Rue Mouassine; tel: 0524 42 97 28; daily L, D; map E4
La Terrasse des Epices; 15 Souk Cherifia; tel: 0524 37 59 04; daily L, D; map E4

Discover Souk Cherifia – a contemporary boutique collective

Beneath Terraces des Epices, at the northern edge of the souks, is the next generation of Marrakech shopping experiences. **Souk Cherifia,** or 'Gallery of Creatives', is a pretty, split-level courtyard space that houses 20 quirky shops which take the very best of Moroccan design – be that a lantern, a piece of jewellery, or a kaftan – and work in modern twists that draw inspiration from around the world.

There is certainly nothing mundane here; it's all about one-off, bespoke pieces that you won't find anywhere else. **Original Marrakech** has beautiful customisable straw baskets, hats, bottle-holders, and lights all created by local women; **Kamal** sells beautiful china and glassware from La Terraces des Epices, children's toys, canvas bags, and t-shirts designed by Hassan Hajjaj and José Levy, with profits going to ALCS which fights Aids in Marrakech; **Erebya Paris** stocks stunning silk kaftans; while **Hanout** sells handmade embroidered kaftans, kilim boots, tunics, and dresses. **Virginie W** has colourful accessories and jewellery inspired by traditional Moroccan design. French artist Sylvie Pissard creates elegantly exotic fashion and homewares including ceramic

plates, canvas totes, and cushions printed with Berber women at **Sissi Morocco**. **Mergen Alaoui** is a scented paradise with locally-produced oriental perfumes of musk, amber, jasmine, and vanilla, as well as spa products, and **La Maison de Bahira** specialises in quality linen sheets, bedspreads, tunics, and bathrobes – all created by Marion Théard, who started her career embroidering for Christian Louboutin.

Souk Cherifia; 15 Sidi Abdelaziz, Medina; map E4

Have a sunlit lunch and then cool off in a chic pool

Marrakech is one of the best places in the world for decadent relaxation, with breezy roof terraces and shady courtyards to lounge about in, away from the heat of the sun and the chaos of the city. Many hotels allow non-guests to have lunch and use their pools too.

Riad el Fenn (Derb Moulay Abdullah ben Hezzian, Bab el Ksour; tel: 0524 44 12 10; map D3) is a bohemian yet luxurious boutique hotel. Lunch is fresh, light, and made entirely from local produce. Eat on the roof terrace and take advantage of the plunge pool with sun loungers, towels and Berber straw hats available. There is no charge on top of what you pay for lunch, and the spa and evening rooftop bar are both open to non-residents too.

Les Jardins de la Koutoubia (26 Rue de la Koutoubia; tel: 0524 38 88 00; map D2) is perfectly located right next to Jemaa el Fna. A grand hotel in the style of a huge riad, the elegant pool is shaded by palm trees, and lunch – club sandwiches, Dover sole, pasta – is very good value. There is a 200dh charge per person, and the spa is also available for non-guests to use.

The **Four Seasons Marrakech** (1 Boulevard de la Menara; tel: 0524 35 92 00; map page 126 E1) also lets you use their pool (for a fee), as does **Les Jardins de la Medina** (21 Derb Chtouka, Kasbah; tel: 0524 38 18 51; map page 58 C3) in the Southern Medina (free with lunch or a spa treatment).

Reservations are recommended at all of the above.

Feast like a sultan at one of Marrakech's best Moroccan restaurants

Moroccan food is synonymous with luxurious feasting. In the past, sultans would spend hours eating course after course of intricate dishes that would have taken days to prepare. In spite of the huge amount of food and high prices to match, a traditional Moroccan feast should be at the top of any self-respecting gourmet's list of things to do in Marrakech.

Le Tobsil is considered by many to be the best restaurant in town. The exquisite food, conjured up by talented chef Khadija Mountassamim, includes fragrant pigeon and almond *pastilla*, lamb tagine with dates and figs, and milk *pastilla* with almonds and orange flower water.

Dar Moha dazzles in a different way. In what used to be fashion designer Pierre Balmain's house, owner and chef Mohammed Fedal whips up delectable Moroccan nouvelle cuisine. The dishes are recognisable but have subtle twists: tomatoes and peppers smoked in olive leaves, monkfish *pastilla*, foie gras couscous, and quail tagine. The emphasis here is on a multitude of taste experiences, rather than an overwhelmingly heavy meal. Ensure you reserve a table round the romantic, flower-filled pool in the courtyard.

Pepe Nero, located in a riad once owned by Pasha Thami el Glaoui, is a relative newcomer. Its beautiful courtyard lined with orange trees and filled with lanterns is both grand and intimate, and the seasonal food – 'modern haute cuisine' – fuses Italian and Moroccan flavours.

All three restaurants are at the top end of the price scale (around 1,000dh for two people with wine).

Le Tobsil; 22 Derb Abdallah ben Hessaien; tel: 0524 44 40 52; Wed–Mon D; map D2
Dar Moha; 81 Rue Dar el Bacha; tel: 0524 38 64 00; daily L, D; map C4
Pepe Nero; 17 Derb Cherkaoui, Douar Graoua; tel: 0524 38 90 67; Tue–Sun L, D; map G2

Forget haggling and shop for arts and crafts at the price-set Ensemble Artisanal

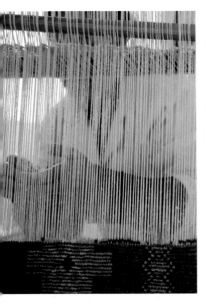

Shopping in Marrakech's souks can be a frustrating and expensive experience. If you have had enough of endless haggling, head to the **Ensemble Artisanal**, which has a fantastic array of Moroccan arts and crafts – everything you find in the souk and more – and, best of all, every item has a price tag, which means there's no haggling required and none of the pestering that can accompany a shopping trip in the souk.

There are Ensemble Artisanals across Morocco; all are government-funded, and everything is made by local craftsmen or brought in from areas specialising in certain craft skills, such as jewellery or pottery. If there are several workshops selling the same thing, it's worth shopping around to make sure you're getting the best price.

Come here to pick up *tadelakt* (polished plaster) bowls and candle holders, terracotta tagines, brass and glass lanterns, carpets, silver Berber jewellery, *passementerie* key chains, leather bags, argan oil, ceramics from Fez and Safi, leather and silk pouffes, kaftans, and jellabas. An added pleasure is being able to watch certain crafts being made. There are lantern-makers hammering out metal and carpet weavers at their looms. If you are interested, they will let you have a go.

Crafty shoppers should come here to check the price of common items and then brave the souks armed with a ballpark figure of what things cost; if you're good at haggling, you should pay less in the souks than at the Ensemble Artisanal.

Ensemble Artisanal; Avenue Mohammed V; tel: 0524 44 35 03; daily 9.30am–noon, 3pm–7pm; map B3

Splurge on an unforgettable evening at the magical Royal Mansour

There are hotels and then there are hotels. The **Royal Mansour**, passionate project of King Mohammed VI, is a celebration of the very best in Moroccan design and craftsmanship and one of the most opulent hotels in the world. No expense was spared in its creation, which took four years and involved thousands of Moroccan artisans. Entry is through a suitably regal four-tonne bronze doorway and in winter a fire roars in a floor-to-ceiling glass chimney. The moody Cigar Bar has black-and-gold enamel walls and the wood-panelled library has a retracting roof and telescope for star-gazing.

Like something out of James Bond, underground tunnels enable staff to move around without disturbing guests. There is also a spa (which non-guests can use), a children's club, and an art gallery.

Best of all, the food. Supervised by 3-star Michelin chef, Yannick Alléno, there are four restaurants: **La Grande Table Marocaine**, serving Moroccan specialities; **La Grande Table Française** – said to be the best French restaurant in Africa; **Le Jardin**, where you can eat al fresco (day passes for 1500dh per person including lunch and use of the pool); and **La Table**, serving simple seasonal food in an outdoor loggia. Eating here isn't cheap, but for foodies – or just to catch a glimpse of this glorious hotel – it is well worth it. Make sure you have a pre-dinner cocktail in the breath-taking Royal Mansour Bar.

Royal Mansour; Rue Abou Abbas el Sebti; tel: 0529 80 80 80; La Grande Table Marocaine daily D; La Grande Table Française Tue–Sun D; Le Jardin daily B, L, D; La Table daily B, L; map A2

Take home a one-of-a-kind Moroccan carpet

For many, a trip to Marrakech isn't complete without buying a carpet. Moroccan carpets are grouped into rural or urban, Berber or Arab. Urban carpets are influenced by the fine designs of the Middle East. Rural Berber carpets are handwoven into abstract patterns and symbols that tell the stories of a tribe. Carpets from the Middle Atlas – **zanafi** – have a deep, woollen pile to keep out the cold and are usually long and narrow. The creamy **shedwi** carpets of the High and Middle Atlas Beni Ourain and Beni Mguild tribes are decorated with simple black or dark brown patterns. The *haouz* carpets of the west have free-floating shapes and bright colours. **Kilims**, or *hanbels*, from Chichaoua, are flat-woven rugs with geometric designs, usually coloured in black, white, and yellow on a red background.

Berber carpets – with their irreverent, free designs – are informal and fun and tend to work well in modern surroundings. As such, certain types – the Beni Ourain and Beni Mguild in particular – have become the height of trendy interiors fashion.

The art of carpet weaving is exclusively female and influenced by pre-Islamic beliefs entrenched in magic and the legends of the Berber tribes. Traditionally, carpets were made solely for personal use. This means that every symbol, motif, and pattern means something special to the weaver – perhaps a wish for fertility, the celebration of a marriage or birth, or an ode to the landscape of a particular region. When you buy a Moroccan carpet, therefore, you are buying a talisman and a unique story.

If you are serious about buying, you must be prepared to spend some time, choosing what you want and negotiating the price. A good carpet seller will be able to tell you the stories behind the patterns and motifs, making your experience all the more enjoyable. If you immerse yourself in the process, and stick to your budget, you will walk away not only with a carpet that you love, but also with an authentic piece of Moroccan folklore.

One of the best places to buy carpets is in the old slave market, or **La Criée Berbère** (map F3) off the Spice Square, an exotic covered warren of dozens of small carpet shops.

Soufiane Zarib is a third-generation carpet dealer whose riad boutique is piled high with wedding blankets, Beni Ourains, and contemporary rugs of his own design. It is where those in the know (including Ralph Lauren) shop for the carpet of their dreams. Soufiane's boutique is in La Criée Berbère, but you'll need to call and schedule an appointment in advance (+212 661 853 487); he will provide directions on your arrival. Similarly, **Lahandira** (44 Biadine, Rue Rahba Kadima; tel: 0524 37 56 25; map F3) has an excellent collection. All good dealers will ship worldwide.

In Guéliz, **Ben Rahal** (map page 106 D3), also has a fine collection of antique pieces. Visit the lovely little **Musée Boucharouite** (107 Derb al Cadi; tel: 0524 38 38 87; map G3) to see a beautiful assortment of lesser-known Boucharouite 'rag rugs'. It also has a café on the roof terrace.

Eat a mouth-watering Marrakchi speciality... slow roast lamb

Méchoui (the word comes from the Arabic *sawa*, which means 'roasted on a fire') is a succulent, crispy, intensely-flavoured slow roast lamb that is a speciality of North African cuisine. In Morocco, the lamb is heavily spiced and then suspended whole (including head, skin, and organs) in a clay underground oven and cooked for an entire day, during which the meat is slowly turned and basted in butter.

Traditionally, *méchoui* was prepared for special occasions, such as weddings, where guests of honour would be served the choicest bits (eyes, grain-filled intestines, cheeks), but these days it can also be found in a few spots in the medina. **Méchoui Alley** (map F2) is one of the best-kept foodie secrets in Marrakech, full of locals but very few tourists. Place your order and the chef will remove the lamb from the oven, tear off a few select chunks, fling it onto a plate, sprinkle it with salt and cumin, and serve it with a hunk of fresh bread. Be prepared to get messy – eating *méchoui* should only be done with your fingers, for maximum flavour impact, and to show how easily the meat falls off the bone.

For die-hard vegetarians, head to the first vegan, vegetarian, and organic café in Marrakech – the **Earth Café**, where all produce comes from a local farm (7 Derb Zawak, Rue Riad Zitoun el Kedim; tel: 0661 28 94 02; daily L, D; map F1).

Discover a secret garden in the heart of the medina

In the Islamic world, gardens are earthly expressions of paradise, where elements of shade, water, and foliage combine to bring both physical and spiritual peace. Marrakech was designed to be a garden city – an 'oasis in the desert' – and though it is justly famed for iconic gardens such as the **Jardin Majorelle** (see page 108) and **Menara Gardens** (see page 129), it is also a city of hidden courtyard gardens that lie at the heart of every riad. **Le Jardin Secret** is an exquisite example of 16th century Saadian art and architecture. Once home to a succession of noble Marrakchi families before falling into a state of disrepair, the palace and garden were restored in 2008 and opened to the public – for the first time in history – in 2016.

Today, the gardens have been divided into an exotic garden, with flora from across the world, and an Islamic garden which follows the original 18th-century layout of four parts designed along rigid geometric rules – a metaphor for Islamic order triumphing over the wildness of nature. The ornate buildings and pavilions surrounding the garden, with their polished plaster (*tadelakt*) walls, inlaid cedar wood doors, *zellige* tiles from Fez, and hand-carved stucco friezes, symbolise the wealth and stature of the original owners. There is also a private hammam and, uniquely, a *koubba* (shrine) and tower which soars as high as many of the city's minarets and from which you can see across the city to the Atlas Mountains.

There is a charming café in the courtyard, offering mint tea, fresh juices and smoothies, salads, pizzas, and sandwiches, as well as a shop selling photographic prints, books, and crafts made exclusively for the museum. There is a charge (for adults) to go up the tower.

Le Jardin Secret; 121 Rue Mouassine; tel: 0524 39 00 40; daily Feb–Mar 9.30am–6.30pm, Apr–Sept 9.30am–7.30pm, Oct–Jan 9.30am–5.30pm; map E4

SOUTHERN MEDINA

Watch Aladdin's lamp being made at Place des Ferblantiers   60

Find your inner Talitha Getty at the best kaftan shops in town   61

Rock the kasbah – at Kosybar, where jazz mingles with the
evening prayer   62

Discover the world of traditional herbal medicine at an
apothecary   63

Be bewitched by the sun-dappled courtyards of
the Bahia Palace   64

Make like a Sultana and float away at Les Bains de Marrakech   66

Wander around foodie heaven in the Mellah Market   67

Step into the Saadian Tombs – an architectural folly
that rivals the Taj Mahal   68

Take some time to hang out at Café Clock   69

Saunter through the historic Agdal Gardens   70

Glimpse the legacy of Jewish Marrakech in the cemetery
and synagogue of the Mellah   71

Enjoy an old-fashioned cocktail in Bar Le Churchill
at La Mamounia   72

Admire the finest Moroccan craftsmanship at Dar Si Said   74

Explore the boutique souk shops along Rue Riad Zitoun el Jdid   75

Imagine bygone days when sultans ruled in the Badi Palace   76

Be dazzled by traditional gold and silver jewellery
at the Grande Bijouterie   78

Travel from Marrakech to Timbuktu at Maison Tiskiwin   79

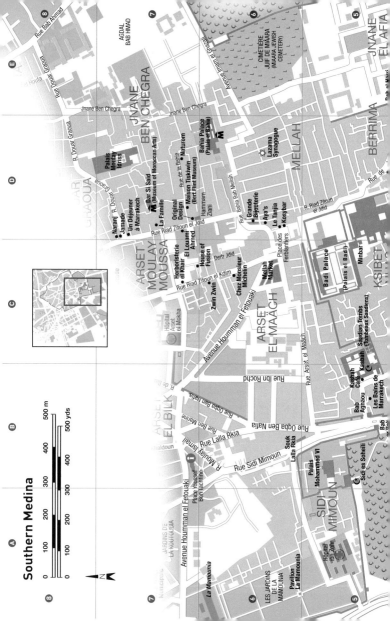

Southern Medina

0   100   200   300   400   500 m

0   100   200   300   400   500 yds

N

A | **B** | **C** | **D** | **E**

Rue Bab Ahmad

Rue Douar Graoua

AGDAL
BAB HMAD

R. Houta

R. Douar Graoua

Jnane Ben Chegra

JNANE
BEN CHEGRA

Jnane Ben Chegra

CIMETIÈRE
JUIF DE MIAÂRA
(MIAARA JEWISH
CEMETERY)

Avenue Imam el Ghazali

JNANE
EL AFIA

Palais Moulay
Idriss

Maraj R. Doura
Jamade
Un Déjeuner
à Marrakech

Dar Si Saïd
(Museum of Moroccan Arts)
La Famille

Original
Design

Rue Riad Zitoun el Jdid

Naturom

Rue In Belbis

Maison Tiskiwin
(Bert Flint Museum)

El Louami
Ahmed

Hammam
Ziani

Bahia Palace
(Palais el Bahia)

Lazama
Synagogue

ARSET
MOULAY
MOUSSA

Herboristerie
el Khair

Zwin Zwin

Rue Riad Zitoun el Kdim

House of
Fusion

Derb Jdid

Chez Monsieur
Michelin

Rue Bahia Bab Mellah

Grande
Bijouterie

Aya's

Le Tanjia

Kosybar

R. Riad Zitoun
el Jdid

MELLAH

Rue de

BERRIMA

Bab el Houta

Place des
Ferblantiers

Mellah
Market

Badi Palace
(Palais el Badi)

Minbar

KSIBET

Hôpital
Arset
el Mokha

Avenue Houmman el Fetouaki

ARSET
EL MAÂCH

Rue Ibn Rochd

Rue Arset el Maâch

Saâdian Tombs
(Tombeaux Saadiens)

Kasbah
Café

Kasbah

Bab
Agnaou

Les Bains de
Marrakech

ARSET
EL BILK

Rue Ben Marine

Rue Oqba Ben Nafia

Rue Lalla Rkia

R. Mouly Ismaïl

Rue Sidi Mimoun

Souk
Lalla Rkia

Bab
r Jdida

Palais
Mohammed VI

SIDI
MIMOUN

Sidi es Soheili

Rue Lalla Rkia

Avenue Houmman el Fetouaki

Place Youssef
Ben Tachfine

JARDINS
DE LA KOUTOUBIA

LES JARDINS
DE LA
MAMOUNIA

Pavillon
La Mamounia

La Mamounia

Hôpital
Ibn Zohr

Ibn Khaldoun

A | **B** | **C** | **D** | **E**

Agdal Gardens **E3**
Aya's **D6**
Badi Palace **C5**
Bahia Palace **D6**
Bains de Marrakech, Les **B5**
Café Clock **C3**
Chez Monsieur Michelin **C6**
Dar Si Said (Museum of Moroccan Arts) **D7**
Famille, La **D7**
Grande Bijouterie **D6**
Herboristerie el Khair **C7**

House of Fusion **C7**
Jamade **D7**
Jardins de la Médina, Les **C3**
Kasbah Café **B5**
Kosybar **D6**
Lazama Synagogue **D6**
Louami Ahmed, El **D7**
Mamounia, La **A6**
Maison Tiskiwin (Bert Flint Museum) **D7**
Mellah Market **C6**

Miaara Jewish Cemetery (Cimetière Juif De Miâara) **E6**
Naranj **D7**
Naturom **D7**
Original Design **D7**
Place des Ferblantiers **D6**
Saadian Tombs **C5**
Tanjia, Le **D6**
Un Déjeuner à Marrakech **D7**
Zwin Zwin **C6**

LES JARDINS DE L'AGDAL

KASBAH

Palais Royal

Grand Méchouar

Pavillon es Saouira

ARSET BAB ER ROB

Nectarame

Rue de Bab Ahmar
Bab er Ryal
Bab el Ahmar
Bab er Rih
Bab el Aghdar
Rue de Bab Ahmar
Rue de. er Rih
Café Clock
Derb Chtouka
Les Jardins de la Médina
Rue ou Méchouar
Derb Chtouka
Rue de la Kasbah
Bab Kasbah
Rue de Bab Imli
Bab Imli
Route de l'Ourika
Avenue Bab. Jdid
Avenue Bab. Jdid
Artisanal
SOHEILI

Watch Aladdin's lamp being made at Place des Ferblantiers

The **Place des Ferblantiers** ('Ironmongers' Square'; map D6) is a fantastically animated square wedged in between the **Mellah** (Jewish Quarter) and **Kasbah**.

Dozens of workshops line this pretty pedestrian space; inside, ironworkers hammer out the intricate lanterns for which Morocco is famous. Hanging from every hook and laid out in front of each workshop are hundreds of their creations: multi-coloured glass, elegant nickel-plated, dramatic iron, and copper that has been punctured into delicate filigree. For anyone wanting to buy their very own Aladdin's lamp, this is the place to come. You will pay less here than you would in the main souks and there is the added advantage of seeing the lamp being made and knowing that your money will go directly to the person who made it. Many workshops will make lamps to order.

As you enter the square from Avenue Houmman el Fetouaki, there are a couple of simple but good tagine restaurants on the right-hand side. Don't be put off by the ramshackle nature of these places – the tagines (cooked on outdoor grills) and simple kefta sandwiches are delicious. To the left, there is a quirkily inventive shop where everything is made out of colourful sardine tins.

The southern edge of the square, where you'll find two popular cafés, **Kosybar** and **Le Tanjia** (see page 62), leads on to the **Badi Palace** (see page 76).

Find your inner Talitha Getty at the best kaftan shops in town

The kaftan, an iconic piece of clothing that was the uniform of choice for bohemians in the 1960s and '70s (think Patrick Lichfield's legendary photograph of Talitha Getty lounging glamorously on a Marrakech rooftop), has experienced a 21st-century revival as boho-chic holiday clothing.

In Morocco, the kaftan is the traditional dress for women; it can be a simple piece of cotton or wool that is worn every day, or a breathtakingly sumptuous work of art that is brought out only on special occasions. Most women still have their kaftans tailor-made, which means you will find tailors and fabric shops in every quarter of the medina.

For those wanting something with a modern edge, **Aya's** is one of the most exclusive kaftan shops in the medina. Nawal al Hriti, the owner and designer, produces exquisitely hand-stitched and embroidered kaftans and tunics of silk, cashmere, and linen in every colour, pattern and style imaginable (for men and kids, too). Inspired by traditional designs, but with modern lines, every piece is a one-off and Nawal also offers a bespoke tailoring service and can produce a kaftan in 3–4 days if she doesn't have many other orders. Prices

start from around £100 for something off-the-peg. She also sells antique postcards of Marrakech, semi-precious jewellery, throws and cushions, *babouches*, and bags.

Norya Ayron (see page 96) and **Topolina** (see page 93) in the Northern Medina both sell quirky takes on the traditional kaftan. Also check out **Kaftan Queen** and **Michèle Baconnier** in Guéliz (see page 111) for wonderfully original styles.

Aya's; 11 Derb Jdid Bab Mellah (just before Place des Ferblantiers); tel: 0524 38 34 28; map D6

Rock the kasbah – at Kosybar, where jazz mingles with the evening prayer

One of the only bars in the medina, **Kosybar** is brilliantly situated on the edge of the Place des Ferblantiers in a wonderful 19th-century riad, with lavish Moroccan-Asian interiors. Adjoining the walls of the Badi Palace, Kosybar has as its neighbours dozens of storks, which are considered a great sign of *baraka*, or luck, to Muslims. At sunset the unusual sound of their clashing bills mixes exotically with the evening call to prayer.

Kosybar is a good spot for lunch, but the most popular time is in the evening, when it becomes lively with expats and tourists. Come early to bag a table on the gorgeous roof terrace, in time to watch the sun fizzle over the medina rooftops. The bar serves great cocktails and the hip restaurant offers delicious Asian-influenced food prepared by Japanese chef, Nao Tamaki. A main course costs from around 100dh.

The owners of Kosybar are part of Morocco's biggest wine-producing family, which explains the interesting wine list. Most evenings there is good live jazz and blues playing downstairs.

Next door is the equally popular restaurant **Le Tanjia**, an 'oriental brasserie' in yet another delightful old riad (with prices which are just a little higher than Kosybar). Seating is on two levels around the pretty courtyard or on the roof terrace, and the menu is a mixture of European and Moroccan, including the namesake dish *tanjia* – richly-flavoured lamb cooked for several hours (usually in the fire of a hammam) in a covered clay pot.

Kosybar; 47 Place des Ferblantiers; tel: 0524 38 03 24; daily until 1am; map D6
Le Tanjia; 14 Derb Jdid; tel: 0524 38 38 36; daily L, D; map D6

Discover the world of traditional herbal medicine at an apothecary

For fans of holistic natural remedies and cosmetics the apothecaries of Morocco are fascinating places to visit. These traditional pharmacies are fun to explore; as well as learning a bit about the medicinal and cosmetic properties of various plants, herbs, and oils, you can buy pampering products or unusual gifts. Essential oils, perfumes, and spices are all great things to take home as fragrant reminders of your trip.

This is also where you can pick up a bottle of **argan oil**. Made from the nut of a tree grown only in southern Morocco, argan – or 'liquid gold' – is a superfood, anti-ageing miracle, and medicine rolled into one. It has twice as much vitamin E as olive oil, is rich in antioxidants and contains omega 6. Used by Moroccans for centuries as a flavouring and cosmetic (an Egyptian botanist in the 13th century first noted its health-giving properties), it is becoming increasingly popular in the west.

As well as the Spice Square (see page 39), there are a few good places in the medina where you can buy bespoke aromatherapy oils, organic perfumes, spice mixtures, natural cosmetics, medicinal teas, incense, dried lavender, and rosebuds: **Herboristerie el Khair** and **Naturom** are both very good. Further afield, see where it all begins at the beautiful organic aromatic gardens of **Nectarome** (see page 150), which also has a shop in the Al Mazar commercial centre on the Route de l'Ourika just outside the Agdal Gardens.

Herboristerie el Khair; 71 Rue Riad Zitoun Jdid; map C7
Naturom; 213 Rue Riad Zitoun Jdid; map D7

63

Be bewitched by the sun-dappled courtyards of the Bahia Palace

The **Bahia Palace** (Palais el Bahia) literally translates as 'the beautiful' and is unique in Morocco as the only royal palace that can be visited. Here you sense how life used to be lived in the days of sultans and courtiers, intrigues, political plots, and, of course, the heights of extravagance.

The Bahia was built in the 1860s by Si Moussa, Grand Vizier (a powerful political advisor) to Sultan Sidi Mohamed Ben Abderrahman, and expanded in the late 1800s by Abu 'Bou' Ahmed, also a Grand Vizier. The latter was the son of an African palace slave but became one of the most powerful men in Morocco when Moulay Abdul Aziz was sultan. According to *the Times* journalist, Walter Harris, Bou Ahmed was, 'a man of no particular intelligence, but of indomitable will, and cruel.' The entire palace took 14 years to build and involved hundreds of the best artisans in Morocco; it is a palace more than fit for a king, attesting to the tremendous wealth and stature of both Si Moussa and Bou Ahmed. Bou Ahmed lived in the Bahia with his four wives and 24 concubines – the empty and, therefore, surprisingly stark harem can still be seen, as can the vast, open-air, marble-paved 'Court of Honour'

surrounded by a carved wooden gallery, where citizens would gather to be heard by the vizier or be handed out draconian punishments.

The Bahia is an extraordinary display of the finest Moroccan craftsmanship and skill, and an example of the period's post-Alhambra style decoration. The series of gardens, once-luxurious apartments, courtyards, and cool reception halls, with their intricate *zellige* floors, painted cedar ceilings, finely carved stucco, and huge carved and painted wooden doors are breath-taking.

When Bou Ahmed died, his once-loyal staff and even his wives and courtesans looted and pillaged the palace, taking everything they could and stripping much of the interiors of their ornament. In the early 20th century, Thami el Glaoui, the notorious warlord and Pasha of Marrakech, used the Bahia as one of his residences and held lavish parties here. When the French Protectorate was established in 1912, Glaoui was evicted and the Governor used it as his main residence. Today it is officially part of the Royal Palace and sections of it, including most of the upstairs rooms, are used by King Mohammed VI for lodging guests. Jackie and Aristotle Onassis once stayed here and hip-hop mogul Sean Combs held an extravagant birthday party in the palace in 2002. In total, the Bahia gardens cover 8 hectares (20 acres) and there are a total of 150 rooms, only a fraction of which can be seen by the public.

Bahia Palace; 5 Rue Riad Zitoun el Jdid; daily 8.45–11.45am, 2.45–5.45pm, Fri 8.30–11.30am, 3–5.45pm; charge; map D6

Make like a Sultana and float away at Les Bains de Marrakech

The art of pampering is long-established in Morocco and stems from the traditional Moroccan bath, or **hammam** (see page 100). Marrakech is full of spas, and no trip to the city is complete without at least one visit. Many hotels and guesthouses have hammams or will be able to arrange for a visit to one nearby.

One of the best is **Les Bains de Marrakech**, a riad in the kasbah that is entirely devoted to luxurious indulgence. This serene place – all muted colours, warm wood, candles and exotic scents – is a blissful escape.

A bonus of this spa is that you can go as a couple. There are joint massage cabins, steam baths with exotic oriental treatments such as sea-salt body scrub with geranium and grapefruit and mint essential-oil body wrap, and hammams where you'll be steamed, soaped, and scrubbed to within an inch of your life. The massages are all tailored and include Shiatsu, the delicious-sounding 'chocolate Zen', a four-handed synchronised oil massage and hot-stone therapy. Argan facials and milk and honey manicures and pedicures are also available. All products used are 100% natural.

Day spa packages start at 850dh and an hour's massage starts at 350dh per person. Tailored packages are also on offer, and a range of luxury products are available for purchase. Book at least two weeks in advance.

Les Bains de Marrakech; 2 Derb Sedra; tel: 0524 38 64 19; www.lesbainsde marrakech.com; daily 9am–8pm; map B5

Wander around foodie heaven in the Mellah Market

The food markets of Morocco are largely overshadowed by their more exotic sisters, the souks, but unjustifiably so. Whether it is a small rural market or something far larger, these markets are where Moroccans come to shop, catch up with gossip, flirt, and do business. This is where the real life of Morocco is played out– something that can be lacking in many places more geared to tourism.

The **Mellah Market** (or Bab es Salam), in the eponymous Jewish quarter of the medina, is one of the oldest in Marrakech. The *mellahs* were ghettoes sectioned off from the rest of the city where the Jewish population lived, and the market was a lifeline for the quarter. Though the Mellah is no longer a ghetto and most of the Jews who lived here have left, there are still reminders of its past in a couple of kosher butchers.

As you enter the huge covered space, you are assailed by the scent of roses, vegetables, and fresh meat. The flowers cascade from stalls just inside the entrance; opposite are a couple of butchers selling legs of lamb, merguez sausages, chicken, and beef. Beyond, there are vegetable stalls with fresh, organic, and seasonal

produce piled like edible jewels. Still further, there are stalls selling preserved lemons, onions and cucumbers, spices, herbs, and olives marinated in a thousand different ways. There is a spice auction every day at 4pm in this section of the market. In addition to food, there are whole areas devoted to the selling of fabrics and two large old *fondouks* (craftsmen's workshops) that now mainly deal in traditional cosmetics and medicinal herbs.

Mellah Market; off Avenue Houmman el Fetouaki; closed Fri; map C6

Step into the Saadian Tombs – an architectural folly that rivals the Taj Mahal

The great Saadian dynasty (1509–1659) ushered in a golden age for Morocco. The Saadians emerged from the Drâa Valley during the 16th century and, on a wave of religious fervour and nationalist sentiment, swept through the country, making Marrakech their capital in 1524. They reached the pinnacle of their wealth and power under Ahmed el Mansour, 'the Victorious' (1578–1603), who built the **Badi Palace** (see page 76) and the **Saadian Tombs** (Tombeaux Saadiens).

The Saadian Tombs were built on the site of an older cemetery reserved for descendants of the Prophet. After the collapse of the dynasty, the tombs were bricked up in the late 17th century by Moulay Ismail, who destroyed Badi Palace but out of superstition left the tombs intact; they were only rediscovered by a French aerial survey of the medina in 1917.

The two main mausoleums consist of 66 tombs inside and a further 100 outside in the gardens. Of the two, Ahmed el Mansour's mausoleum – with its soaring vaulted roof, intricate carved stucco and cedar wood detail and *zellige* tiling – is the most beautiful. Both are stylistic echoes of the Alhambra in Granada, which was built 200 years earlier. The first marble-floored hall of Mansour's mausoleum houses the tombs of several Saadians, including the 'mad' sultan, Moulay Yazid. At the back is the stunning hall of twelve columns, where the tomb of el Mansour is found.

To appreciate the beauty and peace of the tombs, it is best to visit in the early morning. Then head to the lovely roof terrace of the **Kasbah Café** (opposite) for lunch and a spectacular view over the medina.

Saadian Tombs; off Rue de la Kasbah; daily 8.30–11.45am, 2.30–5.45pm; charge; map C5
Kasbah Café; Rue de la Kasbah, opposite the Saadian Tombs; tel: 0524 38 26 25; daily L, D; map B5

Take some time to hang out at Café Clock

Café Clock is not just a café but an immersive experience. The original is a popular hangout in Fez, and ever since its owner, Mike Richardson, established this Marrakech sibling in 2014, eccentric Café Clock has become the hub of the city's creative and social scene. The walls are hung with dynamic works by young Moroccan artists, there are heaving bookshelves by the bar, and there's a cushion-covered roof terrace. On any given day or night, you will find henna painters on the roof, jam sessions in the courtyard, or storytellers in one of the salons. The programme of events and exhibitions is one of the best in Marrakech: there are weekly *hikayat* or storytelling sessions in both Arabic and English, regular musical nights, sunset concerts, weekly yoga and pilates sessions, plus calligraphy and *oud* workshops.

Café Clock is famous for its camel burgers, but if that's a step too far, the rest of the menu has a good mix of Moroccan and European dishes – from *harira* to gazpacho, *pastilla* to aubergine quiche, and salad with figs and blue cheese. Vegetarian and gluten-free options are available.

In fact, the food at this place is so good that it has its own cookbook (*Clock Book* by Tara Stevens) and a cookery school (600dh per person).

Café Clock; 224 Derb Chtouka; tel: 0524 37 83 67; www.cafeclock.com; daily B, L, D; map C3

Saunter through the historic Agdal Gardens

On summer Sundays hundreds of Marrakchi families head to the **Agdal Gardens** for a favourite Moroccan pastime: picnicking. In Islam, gardens are worldly suggestions of paradise – it was this romantic promise that drew artists such as Matisse and Delacroix to Morocco.

The vast Agdal Gardens (agdal means 'walled meadow' in Berber), covering an area of nearly two square miles (5 sq km), were first created as an orchard in the 12th century; renovated by the Saadians in the 16th century; and expanded into their present form and enclosed by pisé walls by Alaouite Sultan Moulay Abderrahmane in the 19th century. Now a Unesco World Heritage Site, they include hundreds of olive trees as well as pomegranate, fig, orange, lemon, and apricot trees. They are irrigated using tanks and a system of channels feeding water from the High Atlas through the groves. At the end of the largest tank – the *Sahraj el Sana* (Tank of Health) – is the Dar el Hana, built for the sultan to entertain his guests. Another pavilion, the Dar el Beida, was built by Sultan Moulay Hassan to house his harem.

The gardens are located in the grounds of the Royal Palace, so are closed whenever the king is in residence. They are hugely popular with picnicking locals, and although a little scruffy round the edges these days, are still well worth a visit.

Agdal Gardens; Fri and Sun only 9am–sunset; map E3

Glimpse the legacy of Jewish Marrakech in the cemetery and synagogue of the Mellah

Established since the 3rd century, Judaism is the oldest religious denomination to have survived without interruption in Morocco to the present day. However, of the 300,000 Jews in the country before the founding of Israel in 1948, only a few thousand remain. There is a Jewish quarter *or mellah (meaning salt)* in every Moroccan city, which was always built close to the palace so that it could benefit from royal protection. The **Marrakech Mellah** was created in 1558 and is the second oldest in Morocco, after Fez. Judaism – like all faiths – is accorded great respect in Morocco. King Mohammed VI is committed to protecting Jewish heritage and is actively engaged in restoring many Jewish synagogues and neighbourhoods.

The **Jewish cemetery** *(miâara)* and **Lazama Synagogue** are poignant reminders of the community's rich heritage. The cemetery is the largest in Morocco – the original graves date back several centuries, with newer additions layered above. An Arab family lives within the grounds and act as guardians and caretakers. They will let you in and show you around for a small donation. The synagogue is the oldest in Marrakech, built in 1492 by Spanish Jews escaping the Inquisition. An ageing rabbi will show you the peaceful blue and white courtyard and prayer hall, which is decorated with *zellige* Stars of David.

Miaara Jewish Cemetery; Ave Taoulat el Miara; Sun–Thu 9am–5pm, Fri 9am–1pm, closed on Jewish holidays; map E6
Lazama Synagogue; Rue Talmud Torah; Sun–Thu 9am–5pm, Fri 9am–1pm, closed on Jewish holidays; donation; map D6

Festival of Eid
The Jewish faith's Abraham is one of Islam's most important prophets – Ibrahim – and it is in memory of Ibrahim's willingness to sacrifice his son that Muslims sacrifice a sheep every year to mark the festival of Eid el Kebir, following Ramadan.

Enjoy an old-fashioned cocktail in Bar Le Churchill at La Mamounia

La Mamounia is one of the most famous hotels in the world, 'the Dorchester of North Africa' and, once upon a time, the social life and soul of Marrakech. The grounds date back to the 18th century, when the Alaouite Sultan Sidi Mohammed Ben Abdallah gave the gardens as a wedding gift to his son, Mamoun, who used them for glamorous garden parties. La Mamounia opened as a hotel in 1923 – a dazzling example of superior Moroccan craftsmanship and elegant Art Deco design. The hotel reopened in 2009 after an ambitious three-year, multi-million dollar redesign by Jacques Garcia, of Hotel Costes in Paris fame.

The atmospheric **Bar Le Churchill** (the only part of the hotel that wasn't renovated) is the best place to soak up some of La Mamounia's nostalgic old-school glamour. Sipping on your perfectly mixed Martini, you can't help but wonder what secrets the wood-panelled walls have absorbed over the years. Did Churchill himself once recline in that corner, wreathed in cigar smoke? Did Mick Jagger and Keith Richards lounge on the leopard print? Was this once where everyone from Omar Sharif to Franklin D. Roosevelt and Charlie Chaplin to Hitchcock used to let loose, swinging to the jazz piano? La Mamounia is steeped in history: part rock-and-roll, part Arabian Nights, part hippy haze, part gilded royalty.

Unusually, you don't have to stay here to get a little hit. Come for afternoon tea and afterwards wander around the spectacular gardens. Two hundred year-old olives as tall as oak trees tower over immaculate lawns and scented gardens bursting with roses, Barbary figs, Madagascar periwinkles, amaranths, and agaves. Winston Churchill thought these gardens were the 'loveliest spot in the whole world'. There is also an organic vegetable garden with peach, orange, fig, and lime trees, and everything here is used at the three Michelin-supervised restaurants. Make a reservation for dinner at **L'Italien**, **Le Français**, or **Le Marocain**. All three are situated in wonderfully opulent surroundings and combine the best traditions of each cuisine with modern twists – monkfish tagine with fennel and saffron at Le Marocain; cacciatore chicken with seasonal vegetables from the Mamounia garden at L'Italien; and king prawns from Agadir with *pissaladière niçoise* at

Le Français. Alternatively, head to the slightly more relaxed Le Pavillon de la Piscine, which is open for breakfast and Sunday brunch.

Nothing at La Mamounia comes cheap, but if you can, save up and treat yourself. Dress up in your chicest kaftan and pay homage to the grand old lady of Marrakech.

Reservations essential.

La Mamounia; Avenue Bab Jdid; tel: 0524 38 86 00; B, L, D; map A6

La Mamounia's spa

La Mamounia's award-winning Wellness Spa is one of the most decadent in the world. With soaring columns, glimmering marble, and giant lanterns, if you need some serious pampering, this is the place. There are several massage cabins, two hammams, an indoor ozone pool, and a relaxation room. Treatments include natural, organic, and traditional Moroccan therapies. Spa passes are available for 500dh per person.

Admire the finest Moroccan craftsmanship at Dar Si Said

Not only is **Dar Si Said** (the Museum of Moroccan Arts) one of the most beautiful palaces in Marrakech, it also houses one of the most fascinating collections of antique Moroccan art and craftsmanship in the world. Built in the 19th century by Si Said, the brother of the Grand Vizier of Marrakech, Bou Ahmed, who also built the Bahia Palace (see page 64), it was turned into a museum in the 1950s.

Come here to admire classic Moroccan design and architec-ture, outstandingly preserved in a celebration of Morocco's master craftsmen (*mâalems*).

The ground floor exhibits carved cedar doors, delicate *mashrabiya* screens, and inlaid daggers and other weaponry. On the first and second floors are salons showcas-ing traditional life. Here you will find the precursors to everything you see in the souks: vintage kaftans, Berber jewellery, embroi-dered leather bags and saddles, intricate furniture, carpets from the High Atlas and Deep South, pottery, brass, and silverware. Occasionally, the museum holds exhibitions of modern art.

A couple of streets away is a charming restaurant, **La Famille**, which is great for lunch. With simple whitewashed walls, wooden furniture, and a tree-shaded court-yard, it makes a welcome oasis. The food is delicious – Mediter-ranean, vegetarian, and seasonal – and there is a great shop on the ground floor selling leather goods, wicker baskets, and jewellery.

Dar Si Said; Derb Si Said, Rue Riad Zitoun el Jdid; tel: 0524 38 95 64; Wed–Mon 9am–noon and 3–6pm; charge; map D7
La Famille; 42 Rid Zitoun el Jdid; tel: 0524 38 52 95; Tue–Sun L; map D7

Explore the boutique souk shops along Rue Riad Zitoun el Jdid

Rue Riad Zitoun el Jdid (Street of the New Olive Garden) is one of the most vibrant shopping streets in the medina. Start from Jemaa el Fna and work your way down.

Warda la Mouche (map page 32 F2) creates one-of-a-kind cotton kaftans, metallic sandals, funky bags, and luxury velvet evening kaftans. **El Louami Ahmed** (map D7) has raffia shoes and *babouches*: some dramatically curled at the toe, others striped in a rainbow of colours.

Jamade (map D7) specialises in ceramics – tagine pots, soap dishes, teapots, plates, and tumblers. For music-lovers, there is **Bob's Music** (map page 32 F2), selling Moroccan instruments and albums by local and African artists. Running parallel to this street is quirky **Chez Monsieur Michelin** (map C6), where the French owner makes bags, accessories, hats, and corsets

from recycled tires and inner tubes. A few doors down is **Zwin Zwin** (map C6), which literally means 'pretty pretty' and sells raffia and leather bags, woven bracelets, and espadrilles. There is a popular café on the roof terrace. **Original Design** (map D7) makes lovely linens and slippers embellished with pompoms, as well as bags, *babouches*, and jewellery. When you've shopped till you've dropped, have lunch at **Un Déjeuner à Marrakech**, which has excellent French-Moroccan food and plenty of vegetarian options, or at what has been called the best Lebanese restaurant in Marrakech, **Naranj**.

Un Déjeuner à Marrakech; 2–4 Angle Douar Graoua, Rue Riad Zitoun el Jdid; tel: 0524 37 83 87; daily L, D; map D7
Naranj; 84 Rue Riad Zitoun el Jdid; tel: 0524 38 68 05; Mon–Sat L, D; map D7

Imagine bygone days when sultans ruled in the Badi Palace

The **Badi Palace** (Palais el Badi), which translates as 'the Incomparable' and is also one of the 99 names given to Allah in the Qur'an, was once a palace of outstanding beauty. Today, all that remains are the haunting ruins, but it is still an incredibly atmospheric place to visit, particularly in the late afternoon when the sun casts deep shadows across the russet pisé walls and you can conjure up ghosts of the past, when the palace was inhabited by the sultan, his harem, and opulent court.

The palace was built in the 16th century by the Saadian sultan, Ahmed el Mansour – the greatest of all the Saadian rulers and a powerful and influential leader with a huge army who held sway in Europe's political struggles during the Renaissance period. A glittering symbol of Morocco's power and prestige, the palace was said to have been lavishly decorated with white Italian marble and Sudanese gold. The palace took 25 years to build but, at the hands of Alaouite sultan Moulay Ismail less

than a century later, just 12 years to destroy when he broke it down and took all the precious materials to build his own magnificent palace in Meknes.

The bulk of the Badi is an enormous open courtyard that follows traditional Islamic principles, with four huge sunken gardens filled with olive trees and a fountain in the centre. In the case of the Badi, there is a large rectangular pool with two grand pavilions at either end. Traces of the underground system that watered the garden still remain. Around the courtyard were 360 narrow rooms on two floors and beyond are the ruins of the old stables and a series of dungeons that were used right up to the 20th century as a prison. Efforts are underway to restore parts of the Badi, such as the courtyard pavilions, which house the original *minbar* from the Koutoubia Mosque, from which the imam would lead the faithful in prayer.

Badi Palace; Kasbah; daily 9am–4.30pm; charge; map C5

Be dazzled by traditional gold and silver jewellery at the Grande Bijouterie

The art of the goldsmith is an ancient one. In virtually every major city in the world there were guilds of Jewish goldsmiths, and in every Jewish quarter an area was reserved for the craft of making gold and silver jewellery. In Marrakech, this trade continued right up until the middle of the 20th century. The **Grande Bijouterie**, which is found at the entrance to the Mellah, has only a few Jewish goldsmiths remaining, but this dazzling covered market is still an animated, fully functioning jewellery souk.

The jewellery in the Bijouterie is unlike anything you'll find in the rest of Marrakech, which is largely ethnic Berber and which most urban Moroccan women wouldn't be seen dead wearing. This is serious 'bling' jewellery, the glitzier the better. You'll see heavy gold-plated necklaces, bracelets, and belts worn over kaftans at weddings, and slightly simpler silver pieces inset with semi-precious stones. Delicate filigree rings and bracelets contrast with these, and there are plenty of engraved silver hands of Fatima (a sign of good luck to both Jews and Arabs).

Regardless of whether or not you are in the market for some gold or silver jewellery, a meander through the brightly lit arcades is well worth doing – you may even spot pieces in the making (one of the great excitements in Morocco is seeing things being made in the shops in which they are sold). If you are looking to buy, make sure you know the value of gold and silver as everything here is priced on weight.

Grande Bijouterie; Rue Bab Mellah; daily 9.30am–8pm; map D6

Travel from Marrakech to Timbuktu at Maison Tiskiwin

The **Bert Flint Museum at Maison Tiskiwin** is one of the most inspiring yet least visited places in Marrakech. If there is one museum you choose to visit in the city, make it this one. Bert Flint, a veteran Dutch anthropologist and explorer, first came to Morocco in 1957 and has spent more than 50 years exploring and researching the culture and artistic heritage of this part of North Africa.

Maison Tiskiwin is Flint's beautiful 19th-century home which he transformed into an enlightening exhibition space for Moroccan and Saharan African arts and crafts. The lines between where the house ends and the museum begins are wonderfully blurred – you sense that no other museum will ever quite live up to this.

As well as celebrating simple beauty, the collection illuminates the links between Morocco and sub-Saharan Africa – a connection that is the very essence of Marrakech.

Everything here is arranged geographically. On cultural caravan tracks you trace Flint's journeys across southern Morocco, into Mali and Mauritania, and on to Timbuktu. It is impossible not to be swept into the past, visualising the tribal and nomadic ways of life that mingled along the trans-Saharan caravan routes. Everything is a feast for the eyes: Tuareg artefacts, masks from Mali, an entire Berber tent made from camel hair, antique engraved guns, sculptural wooden spoons, dyed and patterned leather saddle bags, wicker mats from Mauritania, fabrics and textiles, musical instruments... Fittingly, everything has been bequeathed to the people of Morocco, through the Musée de Marrakech (see page 88).

Maison Tiskiwin; 8 Rue de la Bahia; daily 9am–12.30pm and 2.30–6pm; charge; map D7

NORTHERN MEDINA

Spend a peaceful morning at the breath-taking
Madrassa Ben Youssef — 84

Break out of your comfort zone and have lunch at
Marrakech's alternative food stalls — 86

Take a wild ride through a fascinating part of the medina — 87

Sip mint tea in the courtyard of the Musée de Marrakech — 88

Marvel at images of old Marrakech at the Maison
de la Photographie — 89

Learn the secrets of Moroccan cooking at La Maison Arabe — 90

Dine like a Pasha at a romantic riad restaurant — 92

Seek out the chic boutiques on Rue Dar el Bacha — 93

Hunt for treasures at the most spectacular shop
in the medina – a veritable Aladdin's cave — 94

Collect vintage finds in Marrakech's colourful flea market — 95

Eat under the banana trees at a lush garden restaurant — 96

Walk through the courtyard of Zaouia Sidi Bel Abbes,
Marrakech's patron saint — 97

Stroll down Rue Souk Ahl Fes and discover the busy
artisanal life of a *fondouk* — 98

Explore Morocco's living culture at Riad Denise Masson,
the Musée de l'Art de Vivre, and Dar Bellarj — 99

Brave a traditional Marrakech hammam — 100

Watch the world go by at the atmospheric
Chrob ou Chouf Fountain — 102

Visit the Koubba Badiyin, Marrakech's oldest building — 103

18, Le **D2**
Al Kawtar **B1**
Chrob ou Chouf Fountain **E2**
Dar Bellarj **F2**
Dar Yacout **C3**
Dar Zellij **D3**
Foudouk, Le **F2**
Hammam Dar el Bacha **C1**
Hammam de La Rose **D2**
Henna Café **C2**
Jardin and Norya Ayron, Le **E2**

Koubba el Badiyin **E1**
Latitude 31 **C3**
Madrassa Ben Youssef **F2**
Maison de l'Artisanat, La **E3**
Maison Arabe, La **B1**
Maison de la Photographie **F2**
Musée de l'Art de Vivre **E2**
Musée de Marrakech **E/F1**
Mustapha Blaoui **C2**
Place Ben Youssef **E2**
Qoubba Galerie d'Art` **E1**
Riad Denise Masson **C2**
Rue Dar el Bacha **D2**
Souk el Khemis **E5**
Souk Kafe **E1**
Table du Riad, La **C1**
Topolina **D2**
Zaouia Sidi Bel Abbes **D4**

Spend a peaceful morning at the breath-taking Madrassa Ben Youssef

With the exoticism and western-ised glamour of luxury hotels, spas, shops, and restaurants, it is sometimes easy to forget that Marrakech is an Islamic city and one that is also considered to be a holy pilgrimage site.

The lynchpin of daily life is still the mosque, and much basic learning focuses on the Qur'an, which was traditionally taught at a madrassa (religious school). A spectacular remnant of this is the **Madrassa Ben Youssef**. Religious reminders aside, it is also one of the most dazzling examples of Moorish architecture in the world, reminiscent of the Alhambra in Granada and the Alcázar in Seville.

The madrassa was founded during the Merinid era in the 14th century and reconstructed by the Saadians in the 16th century, who expanded it to become the largest madrassa in Morocco in a deliberate attempt to snub the imams of Fez (the spiritual heartland of the country). The madrassa closed down as a school in 1960 and, after restoration, opened to the public in 1982.

The entrance is unremarkable – just another wooden door on a medina street – but it serves to enhance the visual impact upon entering the main courtyard, where a jade green-tiled rectangular pool reflects shining marble, carved cedar wood, lace-like stucco, scalloped archways, and a blue rectangle of sky above. After the rough-edged chaos and noise of the streets outside, the madrassa is an unexpectedly elegant and refined sanctuary. The courtyard leads to a domed prayer hall, richly decorated with flowing Qur'anic inscriptions, *zellige* tilework and the most incredibly intricate stucco ceilings, looking more like stalactites in a white cave. In accordance with the laws of Islam, none of the decorations can depict animals or humans – everything is of a geometric design. Most guides (if you are with one) will encourage you to stand inside the prayer niche here and say something loud to illustrate the remarkable echo created – especially useful for a mullah with the 900 students that were said to have studied here at any one time. Lessons would revolve around learning the Qur'an by heart and on Islamic law and the sciences. Most students would go on to become mullahs, judges, or lawyers.

On the first floor are the crumbling remains of 130 tiny dormitory cells – this is a particularly atmospheric part of the madrassa. Sneak away from the crowds to explore the dusty warren of rooms – some so tiny that you have to crouch low to enter, some of which afford tantalising glimpses into the courtyard below.

Come in the morning, when all is hushed and serene and the early sun highlights the exquisitely disciplined beauty of the place. If you are lucky, you might chance upon a young calligrapher who sometimes sets up a little table in the courtyard and will write your name in swirling letters for a few dirhams.

Madrassa Ben Youssef; just off Rue Souk el Khemis; daily 9am–6pm; charge (combined tickets including the Musée de Marrakech, Koubba, and Madrassa are available); map F2

Break out of your comfort zone and have lunch at Marrakech's alternative food stalls

Eating at a food stall or grabbing a quick bite from a street vendor may not be everyone's cup of tea, but for die-hard foodies and those who want to try the kind of food that locals eat, it shouldn't be missed. The food stalls of the Jemaa el Fna (see page 37) are the obvious ones, but why not be a little more adventurous and – in between museum and madrassa-hopping – stop at the little cluster of *qissaria* stalls around the **Place Ben Youssef** (map E2), just outside the **Musée de Marrakech** (see page 88).

If you're here at breakfast time, try eggs *khli* (eggs with strips of mutton preserved in fat – surprisingly delicious) or *sfinge* (sugary deep-fried doughnuts). At lunchtime, choose anything from snail soup, *brochettes* (kebabs), fried fish, miniature tagines, eggs scrambled with chili and onions, hearty *harira* soup (lentil, chick pea and tomato), or go for the most simple and filling option – boiled eggs or potatoes dipped in cumin and salt and squashed inside a hot wedge of *khobz* (bread).

For all of this and a drink, you'll pay only a few dirhams and while you eat you'll either be charmed by the hectic stallholder or mesmerised by the goings-on around you: this is the heart of the medina, where motorbikes vie with donkeys for space, vendors call out their wares, and goatskins are laid out to dry opposite the Koubba. If you've fallen in love with this style of eating, head to **Chez Bejguéni** in Guéliz (see page 123) for dinner.

Take a wild ride through a fascinating part of the medina

Biking round the medina can be a great way to experience Marrakech, and the northern neighbourhood, a quiet residential quarter suffused with history and traditional life, is a fantastic place to do it.

Enter the medina through the historic gate of **Bab Doukkala** and pedal your way through Rue Bab Doukkala, lined with fruit and vegetable stalls, butchers, and tailors. Continue on to **Rue Dar el Bacha** (see page 93), past the **Koubba el Badiyin** (see page 103), the busy *fondouks* (see page 98), the **Chrob ou Chouf Fountain** (see page 102), and up to **Rue de Bab Taghzout**, a street of tradesmen and food vendors. At the end is an archway that used to mark the northernmost exit of the medina until it was expanded in the 17th century. Through here is the spiritual heart of the city, **Zaouia Sidi Bel Abbes** (see page 97). Then wind your way north to the **Souk el Khemis** (see page 95).

For an even quirkier experience, why not follow the route in a vintage sidecar? **Insiders Experience** offers tours of the medina by an expat who knows the city inside-out and will illuminate hidden gems and secret histories, all while you are comfortably ensconced in his vintage Russian Ural.

Good bikes (including kids' bikes) can be rented from **M2R**. Insiders Experience offers tours from one hour to half a day, starting at £100. Contact www.insiders experience.com.

M2R, Avenue Mohammed V (opposite Bab Nkob); tel: 0661 59 27 14; map page 106 F2

Sip mint tea in the courtyard of the Musée de Marrakech

and 19th-century lithographs and watercolours of Moroccan ports.

The museum has also built up a fantastic collection of contemporary Moroccan art and regularly holds exhibitions and other cultural events in the central courtyard, the beautiful old hammam, and what used to be the kitchens. To top it all off, there is a bookshop selling coffee-table books on Morocco. Once you have absorbed enough art, culture, and architecture, settle down in the lovely sunlit courtyard café with a pot of sweet mint tea and some Moroccan pâtisseries and let it all sink in.

Musée de Marrakech; Place Ben Youssef; tel: 0524 44 18 93; daily 9.30am–6.30pm; charge; map E/F1

The superb **Musée de Marrakech**, situated in the restored 19th-century Mnebhi Palace, was the home of Mehdi Mnebhi, chief advisor to Sultan Abdelaziz (1894–1908), and later of Thami el Glaoui. Today, the museum displays a wonderful collection of ethnographic and archaeological objects; Jewish items, including a Torah, oil lamps and a menorah; Islamic calligraphy; and a collection of 18th-

Mint tea ritual

Mint tea – 'Moroccan whisky', as you will often be told – is the national drink *par excellence*. You will be offered it when you arrive in your hotel, at the end of every meal, and in most shops and stalls you visit. Preparing proper mint tea is a long and ceremonial process, with the intention of extracting maximum flavour. Pouring tea from a height cools the liquid and creates the '*ras*' or head of froth – a sign of good hospitality.

Marvel at images of old Marrakech at the Maison de la Photographie

For 15 years, Patrick Manac'h has collected photographs illustrating the history of Morocco. In an extraordinary private initiative, he – together with Hamid Mergani – has chosen a selection of these works to be displayed at the **Maison de la Photographie**, which opened its doors in 2009. In addition to the permanent collection, the museum displays new exhibitions every few months that serve to illustrate the diversity of Morocco, as seen through the eyes of those who have visited the country.

The museum now holds over 10,000 original photographs, dating from the 1870s to the 1960s, a significant collection of postcards from Marrakech and beyond, the oldest collection of glass negatives on the High Atlas, a selection of documentaries, and a vast library (covering the years 1870–1960), as well as journals, maps, and prints. In total there are three floors of images which range from the Berbers of the High Atlas to traditional Moroccan pisé architecture to the Gnaoua. The third floor is dedicated to the screening of documentaries, such as Daniel Chicault's *Sceneries and Face of the High Atlas* (1957). In addition to their gallery exhibitions, the Maison de la Photographie holds travelling exhibitions around the medina, and in schools and other cultural institutions, as well as supporting educational activities in the High Atlas. There is a lovely roof terrace, with great views and a little café serving light salads and sandwiches, which is a perfect pit stop after a morning's immersion in old Morocco.

Manac'h and Mergani also run the **EcoMusée Berbère** in the Ourika Valley (see page 150) and the **Musée de Mouassine** (see page 45).

Maison de la Photographie; 46 Rue Souk Ahal Fes (follow the signs from the Madrassa Ben Youssef); tel: 0524 38 57 21; www.maisondelaphotographie.ma; daily 9.30am–7pm; charge; map F2

Learn the secrets of Moroccan cooking at La Maison Arabe

For anyone who loves Moroccan food and wishes they could re-create it at home, a cookery class is a must. It may seem simple, but Moroccan cuisine is refined and elaborate, and there is no substitute for a lesson in Morocco itself, taught by a traditional cook.

Classes are mushrooming all over Marrakech, but the place that started the whole trend is **La Maison Arabe**, the first Moroccan restaurant in the medina, which became one of the most popular places to hang out (Winston Churchill and the Queen of Denmark were regulars).

The cookery classes are taught by a *dada* (traditional Moroccan cook) or by a chef from the restaurant. Groups range from two to 10 people with private workshops available, and there is a translator on hand. At the end of the class – at which you will prepare either a starter and main course or main course and dessert – you can enjoy your creations. Classes start at 600dh per person.

House of Fusion, in the Southern Medina, offers cooking classes ranging from rustling up an 8-course lunch to a pastry class. They begin in the morning with a chat about the menu followed by a trip to the local market to choose ingredients. As the name suggests, the food is an inventive fusion of flavours and you get to enjoy the fruits of your labour at the end of the day. Prices start at €80.

At **Les Jardins de la Medina** (Southern Medina, www.lesjardins delamedina.com), lessons are held on one of the hotel's roof terraces and are tailored to your personal tastes. The standard cookery course includes the preparation of fresh *beldi* (country) bread, different Moroccan salads, an elaborate tagine, and Moroccan pâtisserie, as well as the ritual of mint tea-making. Lunch with wine is included in the 765dh price.

Café Clock (see page 69) also offers fun classes.

If you don't fancy cooking yourself but still want a culinary experience, why not try a food tour... **Tasting Marrakech** offers private, tailor-made evening tours around the food stalls of Jemaa el Fna (see page 37) and spice souks. The tours are run by a Canadian expat and a local Moroccan guide, and can be customised for families with children. The three-hour tour includes a four-course menu and drinks. Similarly, **Mar-**

rakech Food Tours guide small groups around the lesser-known food stalls of the medina, where savvy locals eat. They also offer a 'Gourmet Food Tour': a curated menu in collaboration with a selection of riads, each hosting a single course. Guests are shuttled between the riads in tuk tuks. If you are in Marrakech during Ramadan, they also offer the chance to see how Moroccan families break their fast, at an evening *ftour* – a truly unique experience.

La Maison Arabe; 1 Derb Assehbé, Bab Doukkala; tel: 0524 38 70 10; www.la maisonarabe.com; map B1
Les Jardins de la Medina; 21 Derb Chtouka; tel: 0524 38 18 51; www.les jardinsdelamedina.com; map page 58 C3
House of Fusion; Derb Jdid 81, Rue Riad Zitoun el Kedim; tel: 0624 66 75 67; www.houseoffusionmarrakech.com; map page 58 C7
Tasting Marrakech; www.tasting-marrakech.com
Marrakech Food Tours; www.marrakech foodtours.com

Dine like a Pasha at a romantic riad restaurant

Marrakech is one of the most romantic cities in the world and dinner in a riad restaurant is a dreamy experience.

Dar Yacout (pictured), in one of the most enchanting riads in the medina, is where royalty and movie stars hang out. Candle-filled lanterns illuminate private salons with fireplaces and hidden corners with carved cedar ceilings. Cocktails are served on the roof and the deliciously extravagant food is eaten around the courtyard pool or an opulent dining room.

Through a labyrinth-like warren, you'll find **Dar Zellij** in a stunning 17th-century riad. Tables strewn with rose petals are arranged around a marble fountain. Feast on crispy *briouats*, fish *pastilla*, lamb tagine with figs, or a Marrakchi *tanjia* (slow-roasted lamb). They also offer brunch on Sundays, plus vegetarian and taster menus.

La Table du Riad is all about fine dining with a farm-to-table, seasonal ethos. It has just eleven tables, romantically situated either on the roof terrace, which overlooks the elegant roofline of Dar el Bacha – Pasha Thami el Glaoui's palace – or in the pretty courtyard. Chef Mustapha el Bachna offers an à la carte menu, serving pared-back takes on traditional Moroccan food, and a set fine-dining menu where you can sample his exquisite pairing of Moroccan classics with a Mediterranean twist. Vegetarians are well catered for.

All three restaurants serve three course meals for around 1,000dh for two.

Dar Yacout; 79 Derb Sidi Ahmed Soussi, Bab Doukkala; tel: 0524 38 29 29; Tue–Sun D; map C3
Dar Zellij; 1 Kaasour Sidi Ben Slimane; tel: 0524 38 26 27; Br Sun from 10am, L Fri–Sun, D Wed–Mon; map D3
La Table du Riad (at Riad 72); 72 Arset Awzel, Bab Doukkala; tel: 0524 38 76 29; daily L, D; map C1

Seek out the chic boutiques on Rue Dar el Bacha

Marrakech is full of surprises when it comes to shopping, and the upscale **Rue Dar el Bacha** (or Route Sidi Abdelaziz, as it is sometimes called; map D2) is one of them. This pretty street curves around **Dar el Bacha**, Pasha Glaoui's old palace that is now used for the king's guests (closed to the public).

Zimroda (no.128) is bursting with an amazing collection of antiques, curiosities, jewellery, and pottery. The **Khalid Art Gallery** (no.14) is one of the most respected antique shops in town. There are inlaid ivory chests, silver perfume bottles, ceramics from the Sahara, textiles, and French antiques. Rumour has it that the king himself shops here.

The **Librarie Dar el Bacha** (no.2) stocks beautiful tomes on Moroccan art, literature and food (mainly in French).

Couture pattern-maker Isabelle **Topolina** (no.134) has turned her talents to creating a collection of vibrant, totally unique womenswear using textiles from across Africa as well as reconstructed vintage fabrics. Her eye-catching dresses, kaftans, coats, and tasselled slippers have gained a cult following.

Further along, towards the souks, is **Max & Jan** (14 Rue Amsefah), where their resort-wear, accessories and jewellery have a more toned-down, bohemian-chic aesthetic that takes inspiration from Ibiza and St Tropez (although everything is made in Morocco).

Just off Rue Dar el Bacha (170 Arset Aouzel), Belgian designer Valerie Barkowski's **V. Barkowski** store sells a range of timeless home textiles handmade by Moroccan artisans – all exquisitely displayed against the moody black backdrop of her stylish boutique.

Stop for lunch and a swim at lovely **Dar Donab** (no.53), which used to be part of the Pasha's palace.

Hunt for treasures at the most spectacular shop in the medina – a veritable Aladdin's cave

Behind a heavy wooden studded door, with just the street number as its sign, is a genuine Aladdin's cave of treasures. If you ever wondered where the beautiful lantern, bolt of vintage fabric, or Damascene chest of drawers that adorn your riad came from, the answer is probably **Mustapha Blaoui**.

This is where riad owners, movie set designers, stylists, interior designers, and travellers-in-the-know come to buy the most exquisite things you will find anywhere in Morocco. So popular is it that Blaoui has had to extend his emporium so there is now double the shopping experience.

Mustapha Blaoui hand-picks every piece and commissions every design – he has six workshops in the medina restoring antiques and creating new pieces. Everything works just as well in New York or Paris as it does in a Marrakech riad, and of course the exoticism adds kudos. As a result, Blaoui's book of contacts includes everyone from Oliver Stone to Ridley Scott and the Clintons to Catherine Deneuve.

Come here to buy translucent alabaster vases, rare Uzbek *suzanis* (elaborately embroidered textiles used for decoration), black and white camel-bone mirrors, kilim-covered armchairs, stretched goatskin Fortuny-style lanterns, woven leather chairs and bed heads, wicker mats from Mauritania... But be warned – don't try to haggle. As Blaoui says, 'This isn't the souk!'

Another repository of stylish goodies nearby is **La Maison de l'Artisanat**, which sells accessories, lanterns, and stylish contemporary furniture. Great for gifts or decking out your house.

Mustapha Blaoui; 144 Arset Aouzal, Bab Doukkala; tel: 0524 38 52 40; email: info@ mustaphablaoui.com; map C2
La Maison de l'Artisanat; 70 Bab Taghzout; tel: 0524 37 61 86; map E3

Collect vintage finds in Marrakech's colourful flea market

Marrakech's main souks, north of Jemaa el Fna, are known to everyone, but the city's flea market, which has a fabulously rich seam of vintage treasures spanning a century, as well as some of the city's most interesting craft workshops, is a relatively undiscovered gem.

Souk el Khemis (Thursday market; map E5) is located at the north-eastern corner of the medina and stretches from Bab el Khemis to the northernmost tip. The best entry is at this point. There is just one main artery, running north to south, with smaller alleys leading off it. The main thoroughfare begins with uninteresting everyday items; off to the side, however, are fragrant carpenters' alleys which are fascinating to explore. Here you will find the wonderful reclaimed riad doors and windows (increasingly rare, and expensive) that have become the height of decorative fashion.

Further into the souk (check out the side alleys, off the main drag), come the shops that vintage-lovers will adore. Here you will find everything from Victorian prams, 19th-century oil paintings, and gramophones to 1960s plastic Panton chairs, retro '70s lighting, Art Deco furniture,

African masks, carved Tuareg tent pegs, cast-iron baths, and a scattering of Moroccan art. At the end of the souk are pottery and wicker workshops and a whole emporium selling bowls, plates, and tagine pots, which are much cheaper than in the main souks.

The souk is open every day except Fridays. Thursday is the main market day but also the busiest. Sunday mornings are slightly more peaceful.

Eat under the banana trees at a lush garden restaurant

Café des Epices (see page 39) has always been a popular sanctuary in the heart of the medina; its owner Kamal Laftimi's latest project is wonderful **Le Jardin** – a restored 16th-century riad with a deliciously welcoming garden at its centre. A typically discreet doorway leads into the verdant green *zellige*-tiled courtyard, which is shaded with bamboo, palms, and banana trees hung with lanterns, which cast a gentle glow in the evenings. Colourful piles of fresh fruit and vegetables, jars of olives, and preserved lemons decorate the bar; a tortoise ambles between the tables; canaries chirp; and on the breezy roof terrace there are simple woven hats thoughtfully laid out for hot days.

The menu is a simple, fresh combination of Moroccan and European: 'Niçoise Moroccan' salad with cumin, grilled chicken *brochettes* and sardines, lentil salad, and pigeon *pastilla*. There is a good kids' menu and the bar serves excellent cocktails for an evening aperitif. Some evenings you may find they are screening a classic film under the stars. Best of all is **Norya Ayron's Pop Up Shop** on the ground floor, where you will find her sought-after limited-edition kaftans and accessories in an array of flamboyant prints and colours. Even Kate Moss and Maggie Gyllenhaal are said to be fans...

Another charming garden restaurant in this part of the medina is **Latitude 31**, which serves sophisticated modern Moroccan food. Eat under the lemon trees in the courtyard while the resident DJ plays unobtrusive ambient music.

Le Jardin and Norya Ayron; 32 Souk Sidi Abdelaziz; tel: 0524 37 82 95; daily L, D; map E2
Latitude 31; 186 Rue el Gza; tel: 0524 38 49 34; Mon–Sat D; map C3

Walk through the courtyard of Zaouia Sidi Bel Abbes, Marrakech's patron saint

Marrakech is protected by seven Sufi saints that serve as spiritual guardians of the city. In the 18th century, a *ziara* pilgrimage was instigated whereby pilgrims would visit the tombs of each saint on a specific day of the week. Of these seven saints, **Sidi Bel Abbes** (1130–1205), patron saint of the city, is the most revered. He devoted his life to the less fortunate, and his shrine – the **Zaouia Sidi Bel Abbes** (map D4) – is a symbol of spiritual

Morocco, its magic permeating every corner of this authentic quarter. The complex houses an abattoir, mosque, cemetery, madrassa, and refuge for the blind. Although you can't enter the mosque or shrine, you can walk through the courtyard. Steal a glimpse of the beautiful carved stucco entranceway, the finely painted exterior walls, and the magnificent pyramidal tiled roof. This is about as close as you'll get to the beauty of a Moroccan mosque.

Walking through the courtyard from the Bab Taghzout side – passing an old arcade of jewellers, tailors, and butchers – you will emerge at the riad of legendary designer, **Bill Willis**, who first arrived in the '60s with Paul Getty Jr and stayed until his death in 2010. Chances are that every design detail in the riad in which you are staying was influenced by him.

Guardian saints

The idea of seven saints – es-Sebti – is ancient. It was Sultan Moulay Ismail who brought the tradition into the mainstream. If you take the Tour des Ramparts (see page 38) you will notice seven large stone towers near Bab Doukkala. These are locally known as the 'seven men' and refer to the seven guardian saints of the city.

Stroll down Rue Souk Ahl Fes and discover the busy artisanal life of a *fondouk*

The *fondouks* – or merchants' workshops – of Marrakech are living connections to the old trading and artisanal spirit of the city and are intriguing places to visit. The **Rues Souk Ahl Fes** and **Amsefah** and the streets around Dar el Bacha still have functioning *fondouks* that are as captivating architecturally as they are for what goes on inside. These large riads, centred around a courtyard and decorated surprisingly beautifully, served either as resting places

for travellers and merchants who came from across North Africa to trade in Marrakech, or as warehouses and workshops. In the central courtyards, auctions would be held and the little rooms edging the courtyard served as workshops and storerooms.

Visiting a *fondouk* opens a fascinating window onto old Marrakech, but it's also a great shopping opportunity. Because there is no middleman here and you deal directly with the artisan, you can expect to pay much less than you would in the souks. And buying a piece that has been handmade in front of you makes it that little bit more special.

If you're feeling inspired, why not learn the art of *zellige* tile making, leather and brass work, or pottery from a craftsman in his own workshop? **Atelier d'Ailleurs** (www.ateliersdailleurs.com) organises authentic and imaginative experiences with a variety of traditional craftsmen. Courses start at €35 per person. To top it all off, have dinner in a *fondouk* at one of the loveliest restaurants in town – **Le Fondouk**.

Le Fondouk; 55 Souk al Fes; Kaat Bennahid; tel: 0524 37 81 90; Thu-Tue D; map F2

Explore Morocco's living culture at Riad Denise Masson, the Musée de l'Art de Vivre, and Dar Bellarj

Marrakech is a magnet for extraordinary people and Denise Masson was one of them. The 'Dame of Marrakech' lived in the city for 60 years. Through her understanding of Arab culture, she was a remarkable example of the positive side of the Franco-Moroccan relationship. On her death, she bequeathed her house to the **Institut Français** and it has been transformed into the **Riad Denise Masson**, a cultural gathering place that is all about building bridges between east and west.

Listen to traditional musicians or a talk on Arab aesthetics in the courtyard; wander through rooms hung with an exhibition of rare early-20th-century photographs of Morocco or the latest paintings from a young local artist.

The **Musée de l'Art de Vivre**, just round the corner, is all about the living culture of Morocco. The ethos of this lovely museum is to provide the traveller with an insight into the heart of Morocco through its art and crafts. At the same time, visitors can discover the art of traditional living in a beautifully restored 19th-century riad. For more living heritage, check out **Dar Bellarj** (pictured), the 'Stork's House', another fascinating venue which hosts exhibitions, workshops, and other cultural events.

Riad Denise Masson; 3 Derb Zemrane; tel: 0524 44 69 30; Tue–Sat 10am–noon, 3–6.30pm; map C2
Musée de l'Art de Vivre; 2 Derb Cherif, Diour Saboun; tel: 0610 408 096; www.museemedina.com; daily, winter 9am–5pm, summer 9am–6pm; map E2
Dar Bellarj; 9 Rue Toulat Zaouiat Lahdar; tel: 0524 44 45 55; Mon–Sat 9.30am–5.30pm, closed Aug; map F2

Brave a traditional Marrakech hammam

The art of the hammam (steam bath/bathhouse) is an ancient and integral part of Moroccan life. Water, which is considered sacred, and cleanliness, are essential elements of Islam. In a part of the world where family and community are everything, the hammam is deeply rooted in everyday communal life. This is where people go to socialise, gossip, make connections, do business, and even arrange marriages. There are hammams throughout the medina; some are basic – a couple of small tiled rooms, announced by a faded 'Sunsilk' sign – and others are hundreds of years old and full of character, with great domed rooms heated by wood fires under the buildings and multi-coloured beams of sunlight filtering through stained glass into the steamy darkness within.

Spas with 'traditional' hammams are everywhere in Marrakech, but a visit to a local hammam is a completely different experience and one that illuminates a side of life you won't see anywhere else. This is particularly so for women. It is a place where veils are shed, and girls and old women alike come to giggle and gossip.

Entry to a local hammam (strictly segregated) is around 10dh. Leave your things in the changing room and take toiletries into the first 'warm' room. This is where you acclimatise to the heat and can collect buckets to fill with water – one cold and one hot. Once accustomed to the heat, move into the second 'hot' room to let your pores open and breathe. Move back to the warm room for your cleanse. This is where you coat yourself in oily black *savon noir* (traditional, 100 percent natural soap made from olive oil, which can usually be bought on-site) and then use your hammam glove to scrape it – and several layers of your skin – off. Purifying *ghassoul* clay masks can also be smothered all over your body at this stage. In most hammams, you can have a massage and a *gommage* (scrub) done for you by an attendant for a few extra dirhams. If it all gets

Hammam checklist
There are a few items you should take with you to a hammam: swimsuit or underwear, towel, shampoo, hammam 'glove', shaving cream and razor for men, flip-flops, and *savon noir* (dark soap available by the scoop in spice shops).

too much, just say 'shwiya afak' (gently, please). At the end of it all, you'll look like and feel as good as a shiny newborn baby.

Of all the local hammams in the medina, the **Hammam Dar el Bacha** is the largest and most atmospheric. Built in the 1930s by Pasha Glaoui, the entrance has a beautiful dome and the internal rooms are paved in Carrara marble and decorated with fine *zellige* tilework and carved cedar. If you want a slightly more refined experience, visit a modern take on the traditional at **Hammam de la Rose**, just round the corner, or indulge at a super luxurious day spa catering solely for tourists (see page 133).

Hammam Dar el Bacha; 20 Rue Fatima Zohra; women: noon–7pm; men: 7.30pm–midnight; map C1
Hammam de la Rose; 130 Dar el Bacha; tel: 0524 44 47 69; map D2

Watch the world go by at the atmospheric Chrob ou Chouf Fountain

In a desert city like Marrakech, water is a precious resource. Amazingly, in spite of this, there are public fountains in every part of the medina, where inhabitants come to replenish their drinking supplies, wash clothes, utensils, even themselves, or just pass the time. Marrakech is threaded by a network of underground water systems and channels that provide for these fountains as well as for mosques and homes.

Wander around the medina and you will spot fountains of all shapes

and sizes, from humble brass taps in the walls of streets to something altogether more majestic, like the **Chrob ou Chouf Fountain** (map E2).

Built in the 16th century during the reign of Ahmed el Mansour, the fountain is one of the most beautiful examples of how important water is to the city. As grand as a palace, an intricately-carved honeycombed cedar arch drips over the fountain, which is crowned with shining green tiles.

An inscription invites passersby to 'chrob ou chouf' – drink and look. Most people now come to this Unesco World Heritage Site to look at it, rather than drink from it, although it is still very much a working fountain. Stop awhile and follow the ebb and flow of the daily hustle and bustle, buzz and clamour of this ever-changing city. Have lunch nearby at the charming **Souk Kafe** (spot it by the giant teapot balancing on its roof) which has fresh, delicious food at decent prices. If you are in the central medina, check out the lovely **Mouassine Fountain** – another great homage to the importance of water in Marrakech.

Souk Kafe; 11 Derb Souk Jeldid, Sidi Abdelaziz; tel: 0524 39 08 31; daily L, D; map E1

Visit the Koubba Badiyin, Marrakech's oldest building

Next to the Musée de Marrakech is an (at first glance) unassuming structure that is easily overlooked. But it is arguably one of the most significant buildings in Marrakech. The **Koubba** is the oldest structure in this ancient city and the only surviving example of Almoravid Marrakech.

The Berber Almoravid dynasty (1060–1147) forged an empire that at its height stretched from Mali and Mauritania into southern Spain and Portugal. In 1062 they founded Marrakech and made it the glittering capital of what was one of the most powerful empires in the world. Unfortunately, nothing – except the Koubba – now remains from their time, because the Almohads (1147–1269) destroyed everything when they conquered the city.

An inscription above the entrance to the Koubba states that, 'I was created for science and prayer by the prince of believers...' Originally built in around 1117, renovated in the 16th and 18th centuries and then buried beneath a newer building, until it was rediscovered in 1948, the Koubba was once part of a larger bathing complex attached to a long-lost mosque. This is where the faithful would come to perform their important ablutions before prayers.

The elegant yet stunningly elaborate detail of the dome's interior is truly beautiful. Stand beneath it, watch the light play across marble that seems to glow from within, and be enveloped by Marrakech's rich and ancient past.

Nearby, the **Qoubba Galerie d'Art**, exhibiting contemporary Moroccan art, is worth a look.

Koubba el Badiyin; daily, May–Sept 9am–7pm, Oct–Apr 9am–6pm; combined tickets including the Musée de Marrakech, Koubba and Madrassa Ben Youssef are available at the Musée and the Madrassa; map E1 Qoubba Galerie d'Art; 91 Souk Talaa; tel: 0524 39 03 71; daily 9am–7pm; map E1

GUÉLIZ

Mosey around Yves Saint Laurent's iconic Jardin Majorelle 108

Spend an afternoon browsing the boutiques for original gifts and trendy fashions 110

Take your pick from the best European restaurants in town 112

Lounge on a rooftop with sunset views and a cocktail 113

People watch at glamorous Grand Café de la Poste 114

Reflect on Marrakech's colonial past at the European Cemetery 115

Eat for a good cause at the Amal Centre 116

Listen to live music on a hot summer night 117

Devote a morning to exploring Marrakech's best art galleries 118

Spice things up and head to an Asian restaurant for lunch 120

Escape the bustle and take a stroll in two tranquil gardens 121

Treat yourself to the best pâtisserie in town 122

Have dinner one evening with the locals at Chez Bejgueni 123

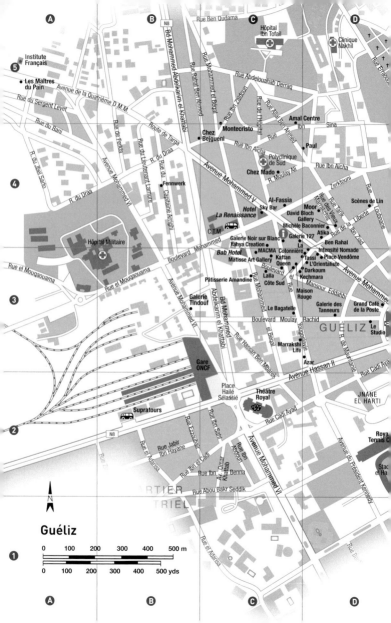

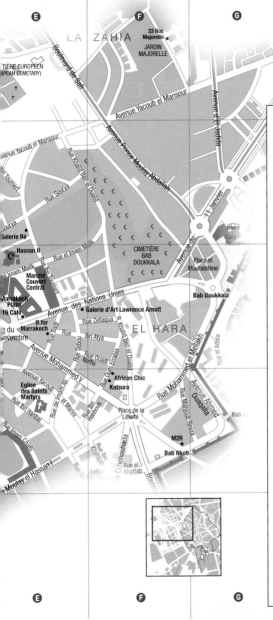

LA ZAHIA

33 Rue Majorelle

JARDIN MAJORELLE

TIÈRE EUROPÉEN
(PEAN CEMETERY)

Boulevard de Safi

Avenue Yacoub el Mansour

Avenue Yacoub el Mansour

Rue et Imam Malik

Rue Souria

Galerie Ré

Hassan II

Rue el Imam Malik

Rue et Toumert

Marché Couvert Central

Marrakech Plaza

16 Café

B.for Marrakech

e du
ovembre

Avenue Mohammed V

Eglise des Saints Martyrs

Rue Ibn Hanbal

Rue Imam Chafi

Moulay el Hassan I

Avenue des Nations Unies

Rue Zellaqua

Ibn Atya

Rue Quadi Erralia

Rue Quadi Nefis

Rue Sebou

Rue Ibn Tall el Merini

Rue Ibn Habbola

Rue Ibn Khaldah

Rue el Echouhuada

Rue el Khattab

Avenue Prince Moulay Abdallah

Rue Khalid Ben el Ouaid

CIMETIÈRE BAB DOUKKALA

Place el Mourabitène

Bab Doukkala

EL HARA

African Chic
Katsura

Place de la Liberté

M2R

Bab Nkob

Avenue du H Janvier

Rue Khalid Ben el Ouaid

Rue el Adila

Rue Mohammed el Mellakh

Rue Ahmed Ouaqaila

Rue Mahboul Amia

Avenue du H Janvier

JNANE BEL ABBÈS

Avenue du H Janvier

Avenue el Fetlida

Gare Routière

Galerie d'Art Lawrence Arnott

Bab

16 Café, Le **E3**
33 Rue Majorelle **F5**
African Chic **F2**
Amal Centre **C5**
Atika **D4**
Azar **D3**
B.for Marrakech **E3**
Bab Hotel **C3**
Bagatelle, Le **C3**
Ben Rahal **D3**
Chez Bejgueni **B4**
Chez Mado **C4**
Cimetière Européen
  (European Cemetary) **E5**
Cotonnière, La **D3**
Côte Sud **C3**
Darkoum **D3**
David Bloch Gallery **D4**
Eglise des Saints Martyrs **E2**
Fennwerk **B4**
Galerie 127 **C4**
Galerie d'Art Lawrence Arnott
  E3
Galerie Noir sur Blanc **C4**
Galerie Ré **E4**
Galerie des Tanneurs **D3**
Galerie Tindouf **B3**
Grand Café de la Poste **D3**
Hotel La Renaissance and
  Sky Bar **C4**
Intensité Nomade **D3**
Jardin Majorelle **F5**
Jnane el Harti **D2**
Kaftan Queen **C3**
Katsura **F2**
Kechmara **C3**
Lalla **C3**
MACMA **C3**
Maîtres du Pain, Les **A5**
Marrakshi Life **C3**
Matisse Art Gallery **C3**
Michèle Baconnier **D4**
Montecristo **C5**
Moor **D4**
M2R **F2**
L'Orientaliste **D3**
Pâtisserie Amandine **C3**
Paul **D4**
Place Vendôme **D3**
Studio, Le **D3**
Tassi **D3**
Yahya Creation **C4**

Mosey around Yves Saint Laurent's iconic Jardin Majorelle

The French painter Jacques Majorelle lived in Marrakech for over 40 years. His art is largely forgotten but the gardens that he designed are world famous. As well as giving his name to the **Jardin Majorelle**, he also gave it to a particular shade of cobalt blue, 'Majorelle blue', which adorns the 1930s Moorish pavilion in the heart of the garden.

Jacques Majorelle died in 1962 and, in 1980, Yves Saint Laurent and his partner, Pierre Bergé, bought the gardens and restored them to their former glory.

There are plants from all five continents here. Wander through the magnificent forest of South Asian bamboo and along curved pathways dotted with bright turquoise and cobalt pots overflowing with geraniums and succulents. There is a cactus garden full of rare specimens from across the world, dozens of different types of palm, from California to the Canaries; and basins, fountains, and ponds brimming with aquatic plants worthy of a Monet painting. Alongside the rush and tinkle of water is the sound of 15 different species of birds which live in the trees. And in a shady corner is a stone memorial to Yves Saint Laurent, who died in 2008 and whose

Yves Saint Laurent

Yves Saint Laurent's passion for Morocco, which spanned more than 20 years, is evident in some of his most beautiful clothes that reflect the rich colours, eclectic influences, and vibrant culture of the country. Reworking the traditional jellaba, kaftan, and *burnous* (long cloak) into chic, flowing, sculptural works of art, YSL managed to encapsulate in fashion what enchanted him about his adopted country.

ashes were scattered here, in the place he so loved.

Having explored outside, visit the blue pavilion, once Majorelle's painting studio and now the **Berber Museum**, which houses Saint Laurent's and Bergé's personal collection of Berber art and artefacts. The exhibition is divided into three parts: daily and ceremonial objects; ornaments and jewellery; and costumes, weapons, woven rugs and carpets, and decorated doors. Opposite is the **Galerie Love**, displaying Saint Laurent's renowned 'LOVE posters'.

The pretty courtyard café is a lovely place to stop for tea or lunch, and there is also a shop selling clothing, books, and Majorelle-oriented trinkets.

Across the road from the Majorelle, check out **33 Rue Majorelle**, (map F5) a concept store selling stylish homewares and clothing from over 60 Moroccan contemporary designers. There is also a gallery featuring vintage furniture and regularly changing artwork, and **Kaowa**, a snack and juice bar. Opposite is **Heritage Berber**, a good clothing and accessories boutique.

Autumn 2017 will see the opening of the **Musée Yves Saint Laurent** next door to the Jardin Majorelle. This 4,000-sq-metre (43,055-sq-ft)

space will be dedicated to a permanent display of Yves Saint Laurent's work – over 5,000 haute-couture garments, 15,000 accessories, and thousands of sketches, collection boards, and photographs. There will also be spaces for temporary exhibitions, an auditorium, research library, café, and restaurant.

Jardin Majorelle; Rue Yves Saint Laurent, off Avenue Yacoub el Mansour; tel: 0524 31 30 47; www.jardinmajorelle.com; daily 1 Oct–30 Apr 8am–5.30pm, 1 May–30 Sept 8am–6pm; map F5

Spend an afternoon browsing the boutiques for original gifts and trendy fashions

Marrakech shopping isn't all about the souks... Guéliz is scattered with many superb contemporary boutiques.

For interiors, **Ben Rahal** (28 Rue de la Liberté; map D3) is where those in the know come to buy carpets. It's a much less hectic experience than the souks and the knowledgeable owner has a fine selection. **Darkoum** (5 Rue de la Liberté; map D3) is a wonderland of antique furniture, African masks, art, ceramics, and textiles sourced from India, Africa, and Asia. For

gifts, go to **Côté Sud** (4 Rue de la Liberté; map C3): hand-painted tea glasses, embroidered tablecloths, candles, and picture frames. Next door is **Maison Rouge**, its sister shop, selling much of the same. **L'Orientaliste** (11–15 Rue de la Liberté; map D3) sells perfumes and oils, antiques, and glassware. **Fennwerk** (148 Boulevard Abdelkarim al Khattabi; map B4) has a sensational collection of Berber rugs and rare fabrics as well as bespoke pieces (appointment only). For intricate and refined contem-

porary Moroccan lanterns that have become world renowned, **Yahya Creation** (61 Rue Yougoslavie, 49 Passage Ghandouri; map C4) is a must. For fashion, **Michèle Baconnier** (6 Rue des Vieux Marrakchis; map D4) has leather ballet pumps, flowing kaftans, fine gold jewellery, and bags to die for. **Kaftan Queen** (61 Rue Yougoslavie, 39–41 Passage Ghandouri; map C3) has elegant kaftans, tunics, and clothes for children. **Intensité Nomade**'s (139 Ave Mohammed V; map D3) glamorous Moroccan fashion is at

the other end of the scale; **Atika** (34 Rue de la Liberté; map D4) has the best leather shoes; and **La Cotonnière** (18 Rue de la Liberté; map D3) sells breezy cotton clothes.

Galerie des Tanneurs (4 Boulevard Moulay Rachid) and **Place Vendôme** (141 Ave Mohammed V; both map D3) have excellent leather and suede bags and jackets. Much-loved **Lalla** (35 Boulevard el Mansour Eddahbi; map C3), Laetitia Trouillet's delicious boutique, is *the* place to go for fantastically chic tasselled leather bags, funky clutches, canvas totes, silk scarves, and necklaces. **Moor** (7 Rue des Vieux Marrakchis; map D4), the sister store of **Akbar Delights** (see page 43), sells sophisticated linen and silk tunics and a beautifully curated collection of homewares.

New York photographer Randall Bachner's **Marrakchi Life** (111 Rue Yougoslavie; map C3), is a relatively new kid on the block, but his minimalist clothes – hand-woven cotton boiler suits, subtly striped tunics, and rough-edged men's shirts – are gaining a cult following. For high-end men and women's clothing with subtle Moroccan influences, check out talented Casablanca designer Karim Tassi's eponymous store, **Tassi** (18 Rue de la Liberté; map D3).

Take your pick from the best European restaurants in town

Having experienced all that Moroccan food has to offer in the medina, Guéliz brings a sometimes welcome respite with some fantastic European restaurants. The only problem you'll have is which to choose…

For classic French food, there is really only one place to go. **Le Bagatelle**, established in 1949 by the current owner's grandmother, is the oldest French restaurant in Marrakech and a much-loved institution that has seen its fair share of colonial intrigues and expat adventures. In the tradition of great brasseries, the food won't disappoint: eggs mimosa, endives with braised ham, duck confit with apples, and veal *ravigote*.

Chez Mado is arguably the best seafood restaurant in town, with fresh fish and seafood delivered daily – notably the famous Oualidia oysters. Everything is cooked to perfection and served in wonderfully simple, cosy surroundings. Excellent French desserts.

Another great French brasserie is atmospheric **Le Studio**. Expect classics such as *escargots de Bourgogne*, *tournedos Rossini* and *Chateaubriand*. They also have a good selection of French and Moroccan wines.

A real expat favourite (and justifiably so) is laidback **Kechmara**, a trendy joint with changing art exhibitions (all artwork is for sale), retro 1960s furniture, and delicious food, such as sautéed octopus, gazpacho, smoked duck-breast salad, great burgers, and tapas (from 6.30pm). There is a fantastic roof terrace – lovely for breezy lunches or cocktails in the evening while the resident DJ plays – and live music every Wednesday, when the place gets packed.

Le Bagatelle; 103 Rue Yougoslavie; tel: 0524 43 02 74; daily L, D; map C3
Chez Mado; 22 Rue Moulay Ali; tel: 0524 42 14 94; Tue–Sun L, D; map C4
Le Studio; 85–87 Boulevard Moulay Rachid; tel: 0524 43 37 00; map D3
Kechmara; 3 Rue de la Liberté; tel: 0524 42 25 32; Mon–Sat B, L, D; map C3

Lounge on a rooftop with sunset views and a cocktail

If you had preconceptions about Marrakech being solely an old city, you will be in for a surprise on a night out in Guéliz. In the medina, everything shuts down by 10pm, but in the Ville Nouvelle, this is when things start waking up. Trendy kids zip through the streets on bikes and gather in groups to flirt and socialise. Music floats out of bars, cafés, and restaurants; the city comes alive. After a day exploring the medina or shopping in Guéliz, what better way to soak up the balmy, star-studded Moroccan night than on a roof terrace with a proper cocktail...

There is absolutely nothing exotic or oriental about the **Bab Hotel**; this is about as urban as it gets. All is chic white minimalism punctured by trendy art and populated by a hip crowd of Marrakchis and expats. The barman mixes arguably the best Martini in town, the music is suitably chilled, and the fabulous Ibiza-style roof terrace is dreamy.

The stylish **Sky Bar** (pictured), on the roof of long-time Marrakech institution, **La Renaissance Hotel**, has the best views in town. Lounge on a sofa opposite a vertiginous plunge pool and gaze over the lights of Marrakech, which abruptly end in a black expanse of desert plain.

With views over the medina, Agdal Gardens, and the Atlas Mountains beyond, the **Sky Lounge at The Pearl Marrakech** is a wonderful place for lunch (around the circular pool) or dinner and cocktails in the evening.

Bab Hotel; Corner of Boulevard el Mansour Eddahbi and Rue Mohammed el Beqal; tel: 0524 43 52 50; daily L, D; map C3
Sky Bar, Hotel La Renaissance; 89 corner of Boulevard Mohammed Zerktouni and Mohammed V; tel 0524 33 77 77; daily B, L, D; map C4
Sky Lounge, The Pearl Marrakech; corner of Avenue Echouhada and Rue des Temples; tel: 0524 42 42 42; map page 126 H1

People watch at glamorous Grand Café de la Poste

The French Protectorate in Morocco, which lasted from 1912 until 1956, had a deep-rooted and long-lasting impact on Moroccan culture. In the early years of the 20th century, Morocco was weak and unstable. Divided by infighting and by the unpopular rule of Alaouite Sultan Abdelhafid, who was considered a puppet of the French, Morocco left itself open to foreign interference. In 1912, the Treaty of Fez brought Morocco under French control and for the next 44 years the fates of both countries were entwined. Today, more French people live in and visit Morocco than any other nationality, and Morocco, in turn, has adopted much that is influenced by French culture.

Nowhere is this legacy more keenly felt than at the ever-popular **Grand Café de la Poste**. As the name suggests, this fantastically characterful restaurant is situated in the old post office and all the original colonial vibe remains: shuttered French windows, faded black and white floor tiles, wooden ceiling fans lazily fanning the leaves of potted palms.

The terrace is where it's at. Grab a table, order brunch (think eggs and bacon, club sandwiches, smoked salmon, and omelettes washed down with fresh orange juice or a Bloody Mary) and people watch to your heart's content. Lunch and dinner are just as good and the bar upstairs is the perfect place to have a pre-dinner drink.

Opposite is the gleaming **Marrakech Plaza**, where you will find a cluster of shops (including Zara) and open-air cafés and restaurants.

Grand Café de la Poste; corner of Boulevard el Mansour Eddahbi and Rue el Imam Malik; tel 0524 43 30 38; daily B, L, D; map D3

Reflect on Marrakech's colonial past at the European Cemetery

Guéliz – the new town built by the French solely for the purposes of their administration during the Protectorate (1912–56) – is full of reminders of the colonial era: restaurants, villas, old hotels... But one of the strongest remnants – and also one of the least-known sites in Marrakech – is the **European Cemetery**, which dates back to 1925. In the heart of this hectic, noisy, and busy modern town the cemetery is an oasis of tranquillity and a surprisingly lovely place to wander round, with its whitewashed tombs overgrown with wild flowers and shaded by towering palm trees.

There are no graves of famous people here, just the men and women who decided to live far away from home. A white obelisk is a reminder of the soldiers who died in North Africa fighting to free France during World War II, an episode recounted in the film *Days of Glory* (2006). The epitaphs trace the history of a colonial power come and gone.

From the cemetery, cross town to Marrakech's only **Catholic church**, built in 1930 and dedicated to six 13th-century Franciscan friars who were beheaded for proselytising (a crime that remains illegal in Morocco to this day). In an unmistakably oriental and Islamic Marrakech, both these places feel intriguingly out of place and are all the more interesting for it.

European Cemetery; Rue Erraouda; daily April–Sept, 7am–7pm and Oct–March 8am–6pm; free; map E5
Eglise des Saints Martyrs; Rue de Imam Ali; free; map E2

Eat for a good cause at the Amal Centre

The acclaimed **Amal Women's Training Centre** is a non-profit organisation dedicated to the empowerment of disadvantaged Moroccan women through imparting culinary skills and restaurant training. The ultimate goal is for these women to become financially and socially secure through the skills they learn. The centre was established in 2012 by Nora Fitzgerald Belahcen, an American-Moroccan who grew up in Morocco and saw a pressing need to help women struggling with poverty, including widows, divorced or single mothers, orphans, child workers, and those with little to no education. It began with a few women baking and selling pastries and has now developed into a fully-fledged restaurant with two locations.

The Amal Centre takes 30 women on every six months for training, while paying them a living wage, and then assists them in finding a job. It has enabled countless women to provide for themselves and their children while escaping lives of poverty and abuse.

The centre offers breakfast, lunch, and cooking classes, and has partnered with several local businesses to offer additional activities, such as yoga, reiki, art therapy, and horse-riding. To top it all off, the homemade food is truly delicious and served up in a delightful courtyard garden. Breakfasts are traditionally Moroccan: local cheese, honey and olive oil, *msimmen* (pancakes), and fresh juices; lunch is usually a fragrant tagine or flavoursome couscous; and dinners are by reservation only, for 20 or more people.

The Amal Women's Training Centre; corner of Rue Allal Ben Ahmed and Rue Ibn Sina; tel: 0524 44 68 96; www.amalnon profit.org; daily B, L, D; map C5

Listen to live music on a hot summer night

The 1960s author and painter Brion Gysin thought hearing the music of Morocco was enough to make anyone become a Muslim. The Rolling Stones didn't go quite that far, but they did dress in jellabas to record the track 'Continental Drift' with Moroccan group, Master Musicians of Jajouka, for their 1989 album *Steel Wheels*. Other ground-breaking bands inspired by the eclectic sounds of Morocco include Led Zeppelin, Jimi Hendrix, Ry Cooder, and The Beatles.

Music is at the heart of every night out in Marrakech and live music is particularly popular.

As well as live music on Wednesday nights at Kechmara (see page 112), **Azar** – a sumptuous Moroccan-Lebanese restaurant and bar – has belly dancing and a string orchestra on most evenings. Ignore the name and check out **African Chic**, where on any given night you will come across young Moroccans dancing the salsa or tango with such style and passion you will think you have walked into a bar in Rio. The live band kick starts every evening and is followed by a DJ. Lavish **Montecristo** has a 'Live Bar' offering high-quality performanc-

es of soul, rock, pop, blues, and jazz, as well as a swanky club and 'Sky Bar'. **Jad Mahal**, **So Bar**, and **Lotus** in Hivernage also stage live music most nights. It's worth noting that nothing gets going in Marrakech until at least 11pm.

Azar; corner of Rue Yougoslavie and Ave Hassan II; tel: 0524 43 09 20; daily; map D3
African Chic; 6 Rue Oum Errabia; tel: 0524 43 14 24; daily; map F2
Montecristo; 20 Rue Ibn Aicha; tel: 0524 43 90 31; daily; map C5

Devote a morning to exploring Marrakech's best art galleries

Moroccan art is experiencing a striking renaissance. Today, it's less about neo-orientalist folk art and more about alternative forms of expression and technique being explored by a young, exciting group of artists. Marrakech is at the forefront of this scene and Guéliz is dotted with some superb galleries.

This renaissance is most widely celebrated during the popular **Marrakech Biennale** (www.marrakech biennale.org), a five-day event established by Vanessa Branson and held every two years in February/March. The festival has events and exhibitions across the city and shows both local and international artists with the intention of bridging cultural gaps through visual art, film, and literature.

In Guéliz, take a morning to gallery-hop between the best the city has to offer. **MACMA** (Musée d'Art et de Culture de Marrakech; 61 Rue Yougoslavie, Passage Ghandouri; map C3) was established in 2016 and has an exceptional collection of Orientalist paintings, antique Moroccan handicrafts, and colonial photography. There is also a wonderful fine-art bookshop.

The **Matisse Art Gallery** (61 Rue Yougoslavie, No. 43 Passage Ghandouri; map C3) is one of the oldest,

and showcases the talents of the next generation. Acclaimed **Galerie Ré** (Residence Al Andalus III, corner of Rues de la Mosquée and Ibn Toumert; map E4) is a glamorous, unapologetically modern space that mixes contemporary painting, sculpture, photography, and installations from Morocco, Europe and the Middle East.

Galerie Tindouf (22 Avenue Mohammed VI; map B3) has a stunning collection of rare Fassi ceramics, precious textiles, Indian miniatures, Islamic calligraphy, and 19th-century French Orientalist painting, as well as revolving exhibitions of contemporary painting and photography.

Super-stylish **Galerie 127** (127 Avenue Mohammed V, 2nd floor; map C4) was the first photography gallery in the Maghreb and the third in Africa when it opened in 2003. Situated in a beautiful 1920s apartment building, the white space with huge French windows places the emphasis on captivating exhibitions by mostly French and Moroccan photographers. It doesn't get more contemporary than the inspiring art at the **David Bloch Gallery** (8 Rue Vieux Marrakchis; map D4), which celebrates street art in particular (hugely popular in Marrakech – keep an eye out for spontaneous exhibitions in disused spaces) and has positioned itself at

the very heart of the contemporary art scene.

Galerie Noir sur Blanc (48 Rue Yougoslavie, 1st floor; map C4) is a dynamic, interactive space with monthly exhibitions and an array of activities from workshops, readings, and book signings to theatre and musical performances. The **Galerie d'Art Lawrence Arnott** (Immeuble el Khalil, Ave des Nations Unies; map F3) began life in London in 1975 and is one of the only spaces devoted to more traditional art in Marrakech. Here you will find figurative paintings by both Moroccan and European artists, including Jacques Majorelle and Hamri.

Spice things up and head to an Asian restaurant for lunch

After a few days of tagines, cous-cous and *pastilla*, you may want a change, so take your lunch at an Asian restaurant.

Katsura is one of the best. The Thai chef whips up mouth-watering Thai and Japanese favourites such as green and red chicken curries, fresh beef, vegetable, and prawn stir fries, and fragrant noodle soups. The sushi, yakitori, and sashimi menus are extensive and good value. Sushi boxes start at 440dh.

Expanding from Ibiza into Mar-rakech, **B.for Marrakech** combines Thai and Japanese flavours for a fresh take on Asian fusion. The service is excellent and the place itself is really welcoming, with trendy design and, as you would expect from an Ibiza institution, great music (including salsa and karaoke nights).

At the other end of the scale, the Hakkasan group has opened **Ling Ling** at the Mandarin Oriental, which is inspired by the philosophy of 'Izakaya', where the food is designed to complement the drinks. Situated on a beautiful open-air terrace overlooking the opulent gardens of the Mandarin, the vibe is buzzy and chic, with sound design mastered by the resident DJ at Hakkasan London. Combine terrific cocktails with delicacies such as Wagyu beef, Peking duck with Prunier caviar, and soft-shell crab. Tasting menus from 280dh.

Katsura; Rue Oum Errabia; tel: 0524 43 43 58; daily L, D; map F2
B.for Marrakech; 4 Rue Badr; tel: 0524 43 00 39; daily L, D; map E3
Ling Ling, Mandarin Oriental; Route du Golf Royal; tel: 0524 29 88 88; daily D; map page 126 D3

Escape the bustle and take a stroll in two tranquil gardens

The Jardin Majorelle may be the most famous, but it is not the only garden escape in the buzzing heart of Guéliz. Grab a picnic from pâtisserie **Paul** (map D4) and while away the afternoon in the cool shade of a swaying palm...

Jnane el Harti (or Parc el Harti) was laid out in the 1930s and is a delightful retreat. Towering palm trees and ancient olives are bisected by pathways, beautifully maintained beds of roses, and fountains. There are plenty of benches to sit, grassy areas perfect for picnics, and even a kids' play area with swings and huge dinosaurs – ideal for climbing.

The **Cyber Parc** is a rather wonderful mix of traditional and modern. Established in the 18th century, this 8-hectare (20-acre) garden was originally built for Prince Moulay Abdesalam and transformed into a botanical garden during the French Protectorate in the 1920s. It fell into disrepair in the late 20th century but was opened to the public in 2005 after a major restoration project. The garden is now divided into two spaces: the traditional, which is shaded with olive, orange, and lemon trees, and the modern, which has open grassy lawns, walkways, and a wonderful array of trees and plants. The park's rather incongruous name comes from its partial use as a cyber space – there is an internet café near the entrance and free Wi-fi at outdoor kiosks throughout the park. A popular place for local families and young Moroccans, this is an oasis of calm for tourists and locals alike.

Jnane el Harti; Rue el Cadi Ayad; daily 8.30am–sunset; map D2
Cyber Parc Arsat Moulay Abdesalam; Avenue Mohammed V; daily 8.30am–sunset; map page 32 B2

Treat yourself to the best pâtisserie in town

Morocco wouldn't be Morocco without its pâtisserie. Of all the things that the French left behind, their pâtisserie is surely the most popular, perhaps due to the Moroccan sweet tooth but also because of the similarity with traditional Moroccan desserts such as *halwa chebbakia* (deep-fried pastry dipped in honey and sesame seeds) and *cornes de gazelles* ('gazelle horns' – pastry filled with almond paste).

Le 16 Café is a stylish place where you can sit on the Marrakech Plaza and watch the world go by. There is all the usual café fare (croque monsieurs, paninis,

and salads), but it's the exquisite pâtisserie that's the real draw: mini fruit tarts, chocolate fondants, *millefeuilles*, chocolate truffles, and honey-soaked baklava. Fill a box to take away with you.

Les Maîtres du Pain is a traditional boulangerie and pâtisserie and the place where all the restaurants – and savvy locals – come to stock up on delicious fresh bread. It's a lovely place to stop for a pot of tea and a cake or *viennoiserie*, too. **Pâtisserie Amandine**, a Marrakech institution since 1997, creates fantastic French pâtisserie that changes with the seasons, as well as Moroccan pastries, both sweet and savoury. Another long-time favourite is **Pâtisserie des Princes**, practically in the shadow of the Koutoubia Mosque (see page 36), which is always packed with people enjoying their wonderful ice-creams, pastries, baklava, and jewel-like Moroccan sweets.

Le 16 Café; 16 Place du 16 Novembre, Marrakech Plaza; daily B, L, D; map E3
Pâtisserie Amandine; 175 Rue Mohamed el Beqal; daily B, L; map C3
Les Maîtres du Pain; 26 Route de Targa; daily B, L; map A5
Pâtisserie des Princes; 32 Rue Bab Agnaou; daily B, L, D; map page 32 E1

Have dinner one evening with the locals at Chez Bejgueni

Few Moroccans can afford to eat out at the sort of restaurant westerners are familiar with. They also know that the best food is cooked at home. There are a few exceptions, however, like the food stalls in Jemaa el Fna (see page 37), the sizzling grills on wheels, and dozens of tiny hole-in-the-wall places serving steaming tagines. Somewhere between these and a more traditional restaurant is **Chez Bejgueni**, a bit of a local legend...

Tucked away down one of the prettiest tree-lined streets in Guéliz, this Marrakech institution is where locals and those in-the-know come to eat. Chez Bejgueni opened in 1973 and is still run today by the founder's son. On a balmy summer's night, there is no lovelier place to soak up a bit of authentic local atmosphere. Sit at one of the tables outside under the trees – be prepared to share – and order whatever looks good that day.

Specialities not to be missed are the kefta sandwich (made with spicy meatballs) – smother it with lashings of the spicy harissa and fresh tomato sauce that come with everything – brochettes, lamb cutlets, and grilled chicken. Salad, seriously good fries, and crusty bread come with everything as well, and drinks are soft. The price varies, but expect to pay around 50dh per person for food and drink.

Chez Bejgueni; Rue Ibn Aicha; daily L, D; map B4

123

HIVERNAGE, MENARA, PALMERAIE, ENVIRONS

Dance till dawn at one of the city's hottest nightclubs   128

Watch the sun set over the enchanting Menara Gardens   129

Leave the city behind and spend the day by the poolside   130

Play tennis in the cool of an early morning   132

Pamper yourself at one of the world's
most sumptuous spas   133

Visit Marrakech's design district for the best
in cutting-edge interiors style   134

Unleash your inner zen at two unique retreats   135

Play a round of golf against the dramatic backdrop
of the High Atlas Mountains   136

Revel in absorbing exhibits at the
Museum of African Contemporary Art Al Maaden   138

See Marrakech from a different perspective on
a hot-air balloon ride   139

Amuse the kids on a fun-filled family day out   140

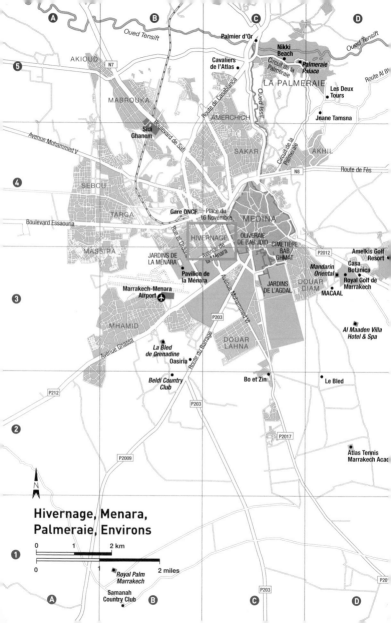

Hivernage, Menara, Palmeraie, Environs

0   1   2 km

0   2 miles

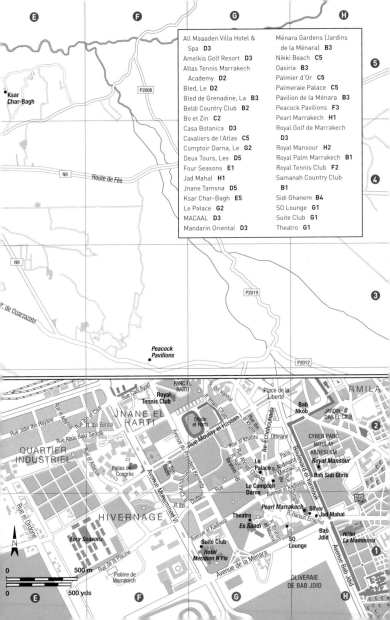

All Maaaden Villa Hotel & Spa **D3**
Amelkis Golf Resort **D3**
Atlas Tennis Marrakech Academy **D2**
Bled, Le **D2**
Bled de Grenadine, La **B3**
Beldi Country Club **B2**
Bo et Zin **C2**
Casa Botanica **D3**
Cavaliers de l'Atlas **C5**
Comptoir Darna, Le **G2**
Deux Tours, Les **D5**
Four Seasons **E1**
Jad Mahal **H1**
Jnane Tamsna **D5**
Ksar Char-Bagh **E5**
Le Palace **G2**
MACAAL **D3**
Mandarin Oriental **D3**

Ménara Gardens (Jardins de la Ménara) **B3**
Nikki Beach **C5**
Oasiria **B3**
Palmier d'Or **C5**
Palmeraie Palace **C5**
Pavilion de la Ménara **B3**
Peacock Pavilions **F3**
Pearl Marrakech **H1**
Royal Golf de Marrakech **D3**
Royal Mansour **H2**
Royal Palm Marrakech **B1**
Royal Tennis Club **F2**
Samanah Country Club **B1**
Sidi Ghanem **B4**
SO Lounge **G1**
Suite Club **G1**
Theatro **G1**

Dance till dawn at one of the city's hottest nightclubs

Marrakech: the new Ibiza...? Maybe not, but the city does have some super-hip nightclubs and bars that stand up to anything Europe has to offer. Marrakech nights are all about high-octane glamour in opulent surroundings, so dress up, hit one of the best venues in town and let your hair down...

For a wild night, try **Theatro** (pictured; Rue Ibrahim el Mazini; tel: 0664 86 03 39; map G1), designed like a theatre, with crazily costumed performers and a good line-up of Moroccan and international DJs.

Other popular venues are the **SO Lounge** (in the Sofitel hotel; Rue Haroun Errachid; tel: 0656 51 50 09; map G1) which stages a mixture of live bands and house music; **Suite Club** (Hôtel le Meridien N'Fis;

Avenue Mohammed VI; tel: 0524 42 07 00; map G1), a more intimate venue for the jet-set crowd, and **Bo et Zin** (Douar Lahna; Route de l'Ourika 3.5km; tel: 0524 38 80 12; map C2), an Asian restaurant in a beautiful garden, which doubles as a classy cocktail hang-out.

Le Palace (Ave Echnouhada and Rue Chaouki; tel: 0524 45 89 01; map G2) impresses with excellent food, a skilled resident DJ, and belly dancing.

Le Comptoir Darna (Ave Echouhada; tel: 0524 43 77 02; map G2), however, is where you'll see the very classiest belly dancing in town, and **Jad Mahal** (10 Rue Harroun Errachid; tel: 0524 43 69 84; map H1) has live music and extravagant food in fabulously opulent, exotic surroundings.

Watch the sun set over the enchanting Menara Gardens

Some 160km (100 miles) from the coast and far below the cooling Atlas Mountains, Marrakech is a furnace in summer. By two in the afternoon the sun's rays are so fierce that the air itself trembles from the onslaught. For Marrakchis, relief is found in dark interiors, private courtyards, and in the city's gardens.

Arguably the most ethereal are the **Menara Gardens and Pavilion**. Created in the 12th century by Almohad sultan, Abd al Mu'min, the gardens are a lovely place to visit, especially between the months of December and April, when the snow-capped Atlas rise up in the distance and are reflected in the rectangular pool that was created as a reservoir (one of the most iconic images of Marrakech). The 16th-century pavilion was used by sultans for summertime escapes and romantic liaisons – legends tell of displeased sultans flinging their courtesans into the reservoir – and was restored by Moulay Abderrahman in the 19th century.

Surrounding this tranquil scene are groves of olive and orange trees which, at weekends, are full of strolling Marrakchis. If you're travelling with kids, there are camels and Shetland ponies outside the gates of the Menara, which can be ridden.

A word of caution – package tourists arrive by the coach load at weekends. If you visit first thing in the morning or in the hour just before the gates close, the light is at its most beautiful and you will have the place virtually to yourself.

Menara Gardens; Avenue de la Menara; daily 8.30am–sunset; free; map B3

Leave the city behind and spend the day by the poolside

Whatever your style, cool off at one of these blissful poolside escapes...

For those who like a bit of glitz and a good people watch, fashionable **Nikki Beach** (of St Tropez and Miami fame; La Palmeraie; tel: 0663 51 99 92; map C5) is all about seeing and being seen. The lake-like pool, surrounded by white day beds, muscled waiters, and thumping dance music, contributes to the party atmosphere – this is definitely not a place to read your book quietly – and the food is also surprisingly good.

If, instead, you want elegance, tranquillity, and luxury, head to the magnificent **Les Deux Tours** – a wonderful villa (also a hotel; Douar Abiad, La Palmeraie; tel: 0524 32 95 25; map D5) that used to be the private home of architect Charles Boccara. In the heart of the Palmeraie, Les Deux Tours nestles in beautifully lush gardens. Delicious lunches are served in a breezy poolside pavilion and there is also a spa.

In the same vein, **Beldi Country Club** (also a hotel, pictured; Km6, Route de Barrage; tel: 0524 38 39 50; map B2) is set in acres of scented rose gardens and has one of the most stunning pools in Marrakech – long and thin, between an avenue of 100 year-old olive trees. Three course lunches at a very reasonable set price are laid on by the pool; the spa, with its own herb garden and all-natural massages, hammams, and facial treatments, is not to be missed, and the wonderful pottery and carpet ateliers at the end of the garden are also worth exploring.

For something a little less extravagant, head to **Le Bled de Grenadine** (Km5, Route de l'aéroport; tel:

0661 45 17 90; map B3). This home-from-home is run by the fantastically friendly Grenadine, who cooks Moroccan-Provençal food fresh from her garden. Donkeys, turtles, dogs, and cats roam the pretty garden and on clear days you can see the Atlas as you float in the pool. Grenadine also rents lovely rooms.

Le Bled (Douar Coucou, Oasis Hassan II; tel: 0608 08 12 12; map D2) is not to be confused with the above, but is similarly charming and refreshingly good value. Lunch usually involves a tagine, a plate of succulent mixed grill, and a selection of Moroccan salads, washed down with a bottle of local rosé. The quirky pool is surrounded by a lilac-painted wall and is a peaceful spot to have a siesta after such indulgences.

Reservations at all of these places are advised. Charges on top of lunch may apply.

Play tennis in the cool of an early morning

If you are a fitness fiend, what could be more exotic than a game of tennis in the shadow of the snow-capped High Atlas? During the winter and spring, temperatures are cool enough to play at any time of day, but in the summer, make sure you head out in the early morning or evening.

Though not technically in this neighbourhood, the oldest – established in 1926 by Hassan II, who loved tennis (and whose photos adorn the walls) – and still arguably the best, is the **Royal Tennis Club** and so must be mentioned here.

There are nine clay courts, four of which are floodlit at night, a pool, restaurant, café, and spectacular views of the High Atlas. Courts cost 100dh an hour and there are teachers for those who want one.

Lessons with a pro, for both kids and adults, can be booked at **Atlas Tennis Marrakech Academy**, which opened in 2015 and has seven clay courts, two hard courts, and one covered, as well as a pool and café.

You don't have to be a guest to take advantage of the stunning courts at the **Four Seasons Marrakech** – two professional-level clay courts, both floodlit for nighttime games. Shoes and rackets are available to rent and there are two professional teachers available for daily private lessons, starting at 1,100dh per person for an hour (350dh for children). Court rental without an instructor is 250dh per hour.

Royal Tennis Club; Rue Oued el Makhazine; tel: 0524 43 19 02; daily 7am–noon and 2.30–10.30pm; map F2
Atlas Tennis Marrakech Academy; Route de l'Ourika, KM 10; tel: 0611 54 66 35; daily 8am–10pm; map D2
Four Seasons; 1 Boulevard de la Menara; tel: 0524 35 92 00; daily 7am–9pm; map E1

Pamper yourself at one of the world's most sumptuous spas

Marrakech's five-star hotels have spas that are the ultimate in glorious self-indulgence.

Ksar Char-Bagh is not only one of the most beautiful places to stay in Marrakech, with one of the finest restaurants, it also has an indescribably lavish hammam. Designed to evoke traditional Turkish steam baths, the marble-clad, vaulted octagonal room is lit only by candles and scented with eucalyptus. A range of oriental therapy facials and massages as well as manicures and pedicures are available.

With 17 treatment rooms, hammams, and a Watsu pool for couples, **Le Spa at the Four Seasons** (pictured) is everything you would expect from this five-star resort. Treatments, inspired by both Middle Eastern and Western traditions, are holistic and organic, and incorporate local plants such as saffron, rose, olive, orange, and argan. You needn't book a room to experience the sublime surroundings of **The Spa at the Royal Mansour**, a vast white haven echoing with soothing birdsong. There are ten private spa cabins offering massages, facials, and hydrotherapy using own brand MarocMaroc, as well as Dr Hauschka and Sisley. There is a hairdressing and beauty salon with Chanel products on top of a Watsu bath, tea lounge, and two hammams.

Clarins opened its first spa in Morocco in 2014 at the **Royal Palm Marrakech**. Designed in the style of a riad, the spa has a tranquil pool, juice bar, yoga room, private garden, sauna, ice bath, and a range of Moroccan-inspired Clarins treatments.

Ksar Char-Bagh; Djnan Abiad, La Palmeraie; tel: 0524 32 92 44; map E5
Le Spa, Four Seasons; Rue de la Piscine; tel: 0524 35 92 00; map E1
The Spa, Royal Mansour; Rue Abou Abbas el Sebti; tel: 0529 80 80 80; map H2
Clarins Spa, Royal Palm Marrakech; Route d'Amizmiz, KM 12; tel: 0524 48 78 00; map B1

Visit Marrakech's design district for the best in cutting-edge interiors style

To find out where the retro lighting, stylish textiles, or quirky furniture in your riad were most likely sourced, head for **Sidi Ghanem**, Marrakech's industrial zone, which has become a destination for cutting-edge interiors and design boutiques. Come here to find pieces that wouldn't look out of place in New York, Paris, or London.

The shops are all handily clustered along the main street and there is a great restaurant, **Le Zinc** (no. 517), which is perfect for lunch and has a little boutique selling leather bags by **M'H** above. **La Maison Fenyadi** (no. 315) encompasses three brands – **Amira**, **Via Notti** and **Akkal** – which specialise in scented candles, chic bed and bath linen, and contemporary ceramics, respectively. **Atelier Laurence Landon** (no. 369) stocks elegant French-designed lighting and furniture with an Art Deco aesthetic. At **Atelier Nihal** (no. 266) Moroccan artisans produce stylish woven bags, cushions, and accessories. **Le Magasin Generale** (no. 369) is a veritable cabinet of curiosities, filled with treasures from around the world: apothecary's cabinets, leather trunks, antique French beds, and African photographs. For contemporary lighting rooted in traditional Moroccan design, head to **Henry Cath** (no.139). **Keros** (no. 238) has perfumes and room fragrances created by Massimo Guadagno and **Natus** (no. 214) is the place to go for 100% natural cosmetics. There are also two contemporary art galleries worth visiting: **Design & Co.** (no. 166) and **Voice Gallery** (no. 366).

Sidi Ghanem is a 20-minute drive from the centre of Marrakech. Hire a driver to take you there and wait, as return taxis are hard to find. Arrange the price in advance.

Quartier Industriel Sidi Ghanem; Route de Safi; map B4

Unleash your inner zen at two unique retreats

Everyone needs an escape once in a while. In Marrakech, there are two very special places that will not only revive you, but give back to the community as well...

Peacock Pavilions is a luxury, eco-friendly boutique hotel in the heart of an olive grove, which the owner and her architect husband have filled with exquisite objects from their travels around the world, bespoke furniture they have designed, romantic Moroccan tents, and vintage textiles, kilims, and carpets (as well as real live peacocks). Peacock Pavilions holds regular – and hugely popular – retreats that involve everything from yoga and mindfulness, mentoring and personal development, pilates and dance retreats to henna and cocktail parties, escorted shopping trips to the souks, wine tastings, and creative design workshops. A percentage of all stays here goes towards **Project Soar** (see page 44).

A combination of inspired design and an inspiring philosophy makes **Jnane Tamsna** (pictured) a captivating place. The beautiful villas, set in a 'lush edible landscape', are like private homes, adorned with antiques and art. The owner, indefatigable Meryanne Loum Martin, organises regular events and retreats here, including literary salons (luminaries such as Esther Freud, Barbara Trapido, and William Dalrymple have attended in the past); cooking classes; yoga workshops (either private or in groups, held in the shade of the carob trees); and nutritionist-led retreats that feature the organic produce grown at Jnane Tamsna and focus on holistic wellness and detoxifying from the inside out. Jnane Tamsna has worked for over 25 years to support community development and environmental conservation in Morocco, so you know that your stay here will not only do you good, but the local community too.

Peacock Pavilions; Km18 Route de Ouarzazate; tel: 0661 213 149; www.3peacockpavilions.com; map F3
Jnane Tamsna; Douar Abiad, La Palmeraie; tel: 0524 32 84 84; www.jnane tamsna.com; map D5

Play a round of golf against the dramatic backdrop of the High Atlas Mountains

Morocco has positioned itself as one of the foremost golfing destinations in the world, and Marrakech is the jewel in the crown. There are dramatic courses set in palm-fringed oases in the shadow of the High Atlas, which enjoy a year-round climate that is sunny and warm (though avoid the months of July and August).

The oldest course in Morocco is the **Royal Golf de Marrakech** (18 holes, par 72). Founded by Pasha Glaoui in 1923, Winston Churchill, David Lloyd George, and Eisenhower have all played here. Ancient eucalyptus, palm, and olive trees edge the course and the High Atlas rise up as the backdrop to most greens. There is a lovely restaurant, too, which is very popular at weekends. Lessons and caddies available.

Created by Robert Trent Jones, the five-star **Palmeraie Palace** (27 holes, par 72) is another stunning course. Extending over 120

hectares (297 acres), this championship-length course has 11 lakes and views to the High Atlas. Each hole has several tees, adapting to players of all levels. The **Amelkis Golf Resort** (18 holes, par 72) includes luxury villas with direct access to the greens and is known as one of the most technically challenging courses in Marrakech.

In the same vein, two further

The king's golf trophy

The Hassan II Golf Trophy, named after the current king's grandfather who was passionate about golf and developed the sport in Morocco, was founded in 1971. It is held every spring in Rabat and attracts top ranking international players.

resorts combine luxury villas with courses: **Samanah Country Club** (a five-star, 300-hectare/741-acre resort with an 18-hole, par-72 golf course) and the **Al Maaden Villa Hotel & Spa** (18 holes, par 72, designed by Kyle Philips).

Rates for all start at around 700dh per day. Visit www.golf-club-marrakech.com for a listing of all the courses in the city.

Royal Golf de Marrakech; Ancienne Route de Ouarzazate; tel: 0524 40 98 28; map D3
Palmeraie Palace; Circuit de la Palmeraie; tel: 0524 36 8766; map C5
Amelkis Golf Resort; Km12, Route de Ourarzazate; tel: 0524 40 44 14; map D3
Samanah Country Club; Route d'Amizmiz; tel: 0524 84 18 84; map B1
Al Maaden Villa Hotel & Spa; Sidi Youssef Ben Ali; tel: 0524 40 68 54; map D3

Revel in absorbing exhibits at the Museum of African Contemporary Art Al Maaden

The **Museum of African Contemporary Art Al Maaden** (MACAAL) opened in 2016, displaying an extraordinary collection of African contemporary art. Its mission is to promote dialogue between cultures and to share art beyond borders.

The museum is a pisé and brick architectural wonder, reminiscent of the kasbahs of old, and is almost as striking as the art within. Helping to illuminate a new vision of Africa, this is a gallery with a voice, where exhibitions visually comment on topical issues. One of the first, which included sculpture, painting, installations, and photography by more than 40 artists, coincided with the 2016 COP22 (UN Climate Change Conference) in Marrakech, focusing on the environment, the relationship between humans and animals, and the exploitation of natural resources.

As well as regularly changing exhibitions, the museum hosts a range of events, from 'jam sessions' to piano concerts. In the grounds, there's also a Sculpture Park: a series of monumental land sculptures by dozens of international artists that stud the Al Maaden golf course (see page 137).

There is a small concept store selling gifts and pieces made by international African designers, and a café on the ground floor of the museum. Entry is 40dh for adults and children under 12 go free. There are daily public tours included with admission.

MACAAL; Al Maaden, Sidi Youssef Ben Ali; tel: 0676 92 44 92; www.macaal.org; Tue–Sun 10am–7pm; map D3

See Marrakech from a different perspective on a hot-air balloon ride

Having explored every inch of Marrakech on foot, by *calèche*, by bike or by taxi, why not try something different? Take to the air and embark on a hot-air balloon ride over the Red City.

Ciel d'Afrique has been going for more than 25 years. You are collected from your hotel by experienced pilot and owner, Maurice (who ballooned across the Sahara), before dawn and driven to the flight area. The sight of the giant multi-coloured balloon – one of the largest in the world – slowly inflating (with air that reaches 100° Celsius) against the early morning sky is breath-taking. As the ropes are released and you float up into the blue you are struck by the beauty of it all: the desert plain, tiny olive and orange groves, 'biblical' Berber villag-

es, and the majestic High Atlas. On landing, you are taken to a Berber village for mint tea and fresh bread dipped in home-made olive oil. For a little extra, take a VIP flight where you have the balloon to yourself and are served champagne.

Marrakech By Air offers a similar service: collection at dawn and transportation to the flight area, where you are involved in the preparations, followed by a cloud-skimming flight. On landing, you are met by the ground crew who set up a tent with a view of the Atlas and serve a traditional breakfast.

Ciel d'Afrique; Imm. Ali, appt. 4, Route de Targa; tel: 0524 43 28 43; www.ciel-dafrique.com
Marrakech By Air; 185 Lalla Haya Targa; tel: 0524 49 07 99; www.marrakechbyair.com

Amuse the kids on a fun-filled family day out

Marrakech is increasingly becoming a family-friendly destination. Aside from the cultural stimulation of the souks and medina, there are plenty of activities that kids of any age will love, all within a few miles of the city.

With 9 million sq metres (3.5 sq miles) of water, 10 hectares (25 acres) of gardens, eight swimming pools, 17 water slides and five restaurants, you could spend a week at **Oasiria** (tel: 0524 38 04 38; daily Apr–Oct 10am–6pm; map B3) and never get bored. One of the vast swimming pools is almost as good as the sea, with waves and artificial beaches; there is a tranquil river ride where you can float through shaded gardens and under bridges on giant inflatable rings; a splash park playground, pirate lagoon, and mini water slides that younger kids will love; as well as an adults-only pool if you need to take a break. All the restaurants are open air and serve everything from barbecues to salads, sandwiches and, of course, plenty of ice-cream. Prices start at 210dh for adults and 130dh for children. Infants go free and there is a free shuttle bus that departs regularly from both Jemaa el Fna and Guéliz (next to MacDonalds).

If you don't have time to travel to the Sahara proper, a **camel trek** in the Palmeraie is the next best thing and an experience kids will never forget. **Le Palmier d'Or** (tel: 0628 956 312; map C5) organises camel rides through the ancient groves of the Palmeraie and there is a café and playground as well. **Dunes and Desert Exploration** (www.dunesanddeserts.com) also offers half-day trips through the Palmeraie for €35 per adult and €15 per child, including hotel collection and drop off.

There are several excellent riding centres if **horse riding** is more your style. **Les Cavaliers de l'Atlas** (tel: 0611 81 68 06; map C5), one of the best, offers half-day excursions or longer day trips to local villages, with lunch, starting from €50 per person for a half day.

For something a little more relaxing, head to the lovely **Casa Botanica** (tel: 0525 06 05 77; daily 8am–5pm; map D3) for lunch. You will spot the brightly coloured awnings of this organic nursery (the first in Morocco) from the road. Inside, weave your way through rows of flowers, trees, plants, and vegetables to the pretty Flower Power Kids Café. Everything here is organic and freshly made by

Aurelia, the owner. There are delicious vegetable tarts, salads, fresh juices, and homemade cakes. While you relax with a pot of tea, there is plenty to amuse the children: rabbits and a couple of donkeys, a charming Wendy house, play kitchen, and several other outdoor play areas.

Les Terres d'Amanar (tel: 0524 43 81 03; map page 144 D6), nestled in the foothills of the Atlas Mountains, is an eco-friendly resort offering zip-lining, tree-top adventures, mountain biking, horse riding, trekking, archery, and craft workshops. If you can't squeeze this all into one day, there's eco-lodges and tented accommodation, as well as a pool and an organic Moroccan restaurant.

If all this isn't enough, you could head off on a quad-biking adventure (see page 158), visit the extraordinary Anima Garden in the Ourika Valley (see page 152), or take older kids white-water rafting along the Ourika River (see page 150).

MARRAKECH REGION

See the real Morocco on a trek through
the magnificent High Atlas — 146

Indulge in a day at a country retreat with unbeatable views — 148

Ski on the highest slopes in Africa and have lunch
in a French chalet — 149

Explore aromatic gardens and Berber museums
in the idyllic Ourika Valley — 150

Let your imagination run wild at André Heller's
charming Anima Gardens — 152

Have lunch by the seven waterfalls of Setti Fatma — 153

Laze by Lake Lalla-Takerkoust, at the foot of the High Atlas — 154

Take to the air on a thrilling helicopter ride — 155

Go glamping and unwind in the majestic Agafay Desert — 156

Speed through palm groves, countryside, and desert
on a quad-biking adventure — 158

Behold the highest waterfalls in Morocco — 159

Drive to enchanting Essaouira for a day by the sea — 160

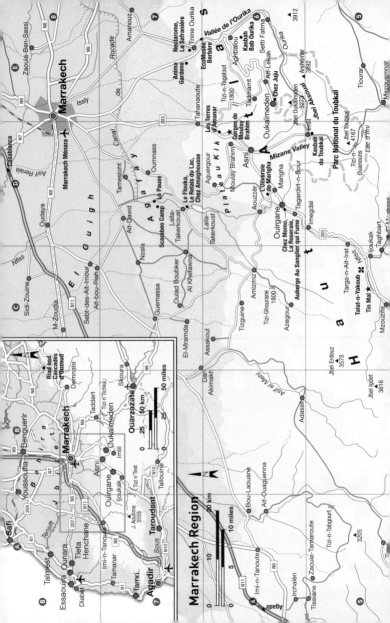

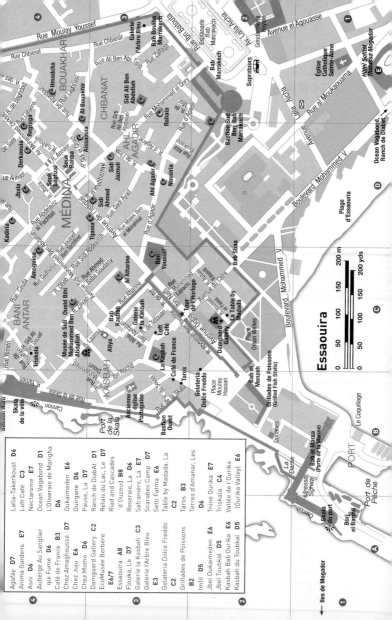

Essaouira

Agafay **D7**
Anima Gardens **E7**
Asni **D6**
Auberge Au Sanglier qui Fume **D6**
Café de France **D7**
Chez Amaghousse **D7**
Chez Juju **E6**
Chez Momo **D6**
Damgaard Gallery **C2**
EcoMusée Berbère **E6/7**
Essaouira **A8**
Flouka, Le **D7**
Galerie la Kasbah **C3**
Galerie l'Arbre Bleu **E3**
Gelateria Dolce Freddo **C2**
Grillades de Poissons **B2**
Imlil **D5**
Jbel Oukaimeden **E6**
Jbel Toubkal **D5**
Kasbah Bab Ourika **E6**
Kasbah du Toubkal **D5**

Lalla-Takerkoust **D6**
Loft Café **E7**
Nectarome **E7**
Ocean Vagabond **D1**
L'Oliveraie de Marigha **D6**
Oukaïmeden **E6**
Ourigane **D6**
Pause, La **D7**
Ranch de DiabAt **D1**
Relais du Lac, Le **D7**
Riad and Cascades d'Ouzoud **B8**
Roseraie, La **D6**
Safranière, La **E7**
Scarabeo Camp **D7**
Setti-Fatma **E6**
Table by Madada, La **C2**
Taros **B3**
Terres d'Amanar, Les **B2**
Tnine Ourika **E7**
Triskala **C4**
Vallée de l'Ourika (Ourika Valley) **E6**

← Iles de Mogador

0   50   100   150   200 m
0   50   100   150   200 yds

See the real Morocco on a trek through the magnificent High Atlas

With many of the most beautiful and culturally interesting places in Morocco being inaccessible by car, trekking and walking are often the best ways to experience the 'true' Morocco. In the High Atlas region you are rewarded by an unhurried pace, can visit places untouched by the modern world, spend time with local people, and see some of the most spectacular scenery in the country.

Just an hour from Marrakech, the monumental High Atlas mountain range is 725km (450 miles) long, with summits over 4,000 metres/13,100ft. Though most come to trek for several days, a day trip is enough to give a tantalising snapshot of a way of life that has changed little in centuries.

The road from Marrakech leads to **Asni** (map D6), where there is a Saturday souk with food and livestock, carpets, fossils, and other local crafts. To the south of Asni towers **Jbel Toubkal** (map D5), at 4,167 metres (13,700ft) the highest mountain in North Africa. The first recorded ascent of Toubkal was not made until 1923 and testifies to the tribal fortress mentality maintained by local Berbers well into the 20th century. But times have changed since then.

Beyond Asni, and in the shadow of Jbel Toubkal, is the rugged village of **Imlil** (map D5), where most treks begin. The best place to base yourself for the day is the magical **Kasbah du Toubkal**, which perches above the town and has such spectacular views that Martin Scorsese filmed his biopic of the Dalai Llama, *Kundun*, here.

The Kasbah organises treks that last from 45 minutes to seven hours. The stunning walks pass through fruit orchards and take in waterfalls, saints' tombs, and mountain villages where you can stop for tea. Return to the Kasbah for a hearty Moroccan lunch (around 150dh). On full-day treks a picnic is provided and you can

spend the night in a village or back at the Kasbah. A percentage of the profits here goes to the Imlil Village Association, which funds essentials like 4x4 ambulances, schools, and clinics.

Other tour companies specialising in treks from Imlil include **Naturally Morocco** (www.naturallymorocco.co.uk) and **Imlil Trek** (www.imliltrek.com), which is run by a fully licensed and experienced Moroccan guide, El Houssain Ait Bahmad. Unless you are an experienced hiker, always hire a guide as few trails are marked and conditions on the mountain can be changeable.

The **Ait Bougmez Valley** (also known as the 'Happy Valley'), around four hours' drive from Marrakech, is another exceptionally beautiful trekking region, and has only recently been opened up to tourists. Treks range from one day to longer overnight itineraries, suited to more experienced climbers, which include an ascent of **Jbel M'goun**, the second-highest mountain in Morocco at 4,071 metres (13,356ft). **Epic Morocco** (www.epicmorocco.co.uk) is another respected company which organises treks here.

Kasbah du Toubkal; Imlil; tel: 0524 48 56 11; www.kasbahdutoubkal.com; daily B, L, D; map D5

Indulge in a day at a country retreat with unbeatable views

In the foothills of the Atlas are several enchanting retreats where you can have lunch, lounge by the pool, or explore the surrounding countryside.

The village of **Ouirgane** (map D6; with a souk on Thursdays) has some of the best places. **Chez Momo** is a hugely popular spot with a lovely pool, sublime views, and a charming garden restaurant serving Moroccan food. In winter, the rustic indoor dining room with a roaring fire is wonderfully cosy. Lunch at **La Roseraie** – seasonal, organic, and locally sourced – is served either by one of three pools or in the cosy restaurant. There is also a spa and hammam, horse-riding, hiking, and water-sports on the nearby reservoir.

The pool of **L'Oliveraie de Marigha**, just outside Ouirgane, is big enough to be a small lake. There are good lunch menus including use of the pool. The **Auberge Au Sanglier qui Fume** is a charming old favourite, with tables under a vine-covered gazebo, delicious French food, a pool, billiards, and mountain biking.

All the sites below: map D6
Auberge Chez Momo; Ouirgane; tel: 0524 48 57 04; daily L, D
La Roseraie; Ouirgane; tel: 052448 56 94; www.laroseraiehotel.com; daily L, D
L'Oliveraie de Marigha; KM 59 Douar Marigha; tel: 0524 48 42 81; www.oliveraie-de-marigha.com; daily L, D
Auberge Au Sanglier qui Fume; Ouirgane; tel: 0524 48 57 07; daily L, D

Ski on the highest slopes in Africa and have lunch in a French chalet

There aren't many places in the world where you can say that you have skied in the morning and sunbathed in the afternoon. The ski resort of **Oukaïmeden** (map E6), an hour from Marrakech (hire a car or take a grand taxi; map E6), sits at 2,650 metres (8,700ft). The season, if there is snow, runs from late December to the end of March and the pistes range from nursery to a rather hairy black run. There is little in the way of piste grooming so conditions can be rough and as rescue services are virtually non-existent and the nearest hospital is in Marrakech, skiing off-piste is inadvisable.

There are seven drag lifts and one chair lift – the highest in North Africa at 3,243 metres (10,640ft) – to the top of **Jbel Oukaïmeden** (map E6). A viewpoint with an orientation table is set at the top, with sweeping views south to Toubkal and northwards to Marrakech. There are prehistoric rock engravings along the north side of the plateau. Ancient skis and boots can be hired from the bottom of the piste and a donkey will carry you and your equipment back from wherever you end up.

On winter weekends, Oukaïmeden becomes packed with Moroccans flinging themselves down the slopes on makeshift toboggans and very

serious French skiers. The skiing here may not be first class, but a day spent in the sparkling mountain air is a wonderful escape from Marrakech. The real draw is **Chez Juju**, a rustic French-style chalet restaurant and hotel. Feast on delectable wild-boar sausage casseroles with bottles of rich red wine and pay no more than 150dh. You could almost be in the Alps if it weren't for the donkeys...

Chez Juju; Auberge de L'Anghour, Oukaimeden; tel: 0524 0524 31 90 05; map E6

Explore aromatic gardens and Berber museums in the idyllic Ourika Valley

The Ourika River, which flows down from the High Atlas, is the lifeblood of Marrakech and the verdant **Ourika Valley** (map E6). With precariously perched Berber villages that haven't changed in centuries, hillsides abundant with fruit trees, and emerald-green terraced fields, it's a delightful country idyll. During summer weekends, the valley is full of picnicking Marrakchis, but this whole area has much that is of interest throughout the year.

The Ourika Valley proper starts 30km from Marrakech and the village of **Tnine Ourika** (map E7) is at its heart. There are several good local restaurants along the main street, where you will also find stalls selling argan oil, fossils, carpets, and jewellery.

Just outside town is **Nectarome**, a beautiful, organic, aromatic garden brimming with over fifty types of medicinal and ornamental local plants. Founded by an aromatherapist, everything here is made into essential oils and natural products, which are sold in the shop. There are workshops centred on beauty, health, and cooking available to visitors, as well as a restaurant serving Moroccan fare. **La Safranière** is a saffron farm, where you can visit the fields, work-

shops, and a little museum to learn about the extraordinary history and culture of the crocus, whose pollen sells like gold dust. The flowering season is in November.

Nearby in the village of **Tafza**, known for its pottery, is the **Eco-Musée Berbère**, run by the same owners as the **Maison de la Photographie** (see page 89) and situated in a traditional pisé building. With the help of the local people, the museum has been filled with a collection of carpets, jewellery, clothing, and pottery. Old photographs are on display and there are documentaries to watch – all illumi-nating the world of the Berbers. The museum also organises walks into the countryside, and visits to pottery workshops and farms. At the end of the valley, just before the High Atlas really begins, is the **Kasbah Bab Ourika**, a stunning eco-friendly hotel and dreamy place to have lunch and a swim. Situated on its very own mini mountain, with some of the most spectacular views in Morocco, the Kasbah has fine food and also organises trekking, camel safaris, mountain biking, and horse riding.

If you want a bit more action and have older kids, why not try **white-water rafting** down the Ourika River. Morocco Rafting (www.rafting.ma) organises two runs a day (March–May) for £70 per person, including gear hire, snacks, and transfers from Jemaa el Fna.

Nectarome; Tnine Ourika Douar Elhaddad; tel: 0524 48 21 49; www.jardin-bioaromatique-ourika.com; daily 9am–5pm; map E7
La Safranière; Ferme Boutouil Takateret, Km34, Tnine Ourika; tel: 0522 48 44 76; daily 8am–6pm; charge; map E7
EcoMusée Berbère; Tafza, Route de l'Ourika, km 37; tel: 0524 38 57 21; daily 9.30am–7pm; map E6/7
Kasbah Bab Ourika; Tnine Ourika; tel: 0668 74 95 47; map E6

Let your imagination run wild at André Heller's charming Anima Gardens

André Heller is one of the world's most celebrated multi-media artists. His latest project is the fantastical, otherworldly **Anima Gardens** in the Ourika Valley – a lush, 2-hectare (5-acre) botanical, art-filled wonderland that flourishes on what was once a barren plot of earth.

Heller created the garden to be a soulful, meditative sanctuary – a place of 'healing, contemplation, and inspiration'. The luxuriant garden, filled with roses, dozens of species of cacti and palm, bamboo

forests, blossoming trees, brightly coloured pavilions, bridges, and fountain-studded lakes is beautiful, but the real draw is to be found in the vibrant sculptures that are scattered like jewels throughout. There are giant conical structures reminiscent of spice pyramids in the souks, African mask-like heads that spout cooling water from their mouths, Chinese zodiac columns, druid stone gardens, and a miniature mirrored playhouse. Surprises are literally around every corner and children, especially, will find this a playful paradise.

There is also a **museum**, which exhibits paintings, photographs, and the works of visual artists from across the world, as well as the kaleidoscopic Paul Bowles Café, which serves fresh juices, pizza, and Moroccan pastries. The garden employs dozens of people from the local community and a portion of the profits is invested in nearby schools.

There is a free shuttle service that departs three times a day from the carpark behind the Koutoubia in Marrakech. Tickets for the garden should be bought in advance.

Anima Gardens; Route del'Ourika; tel: 0524 44 86 58; www.anima-garden.com; daily 9am–5pm; map E7

Have lunch by the seven waterfalls of Setti Fatma

Beyond the **Ourika Valley** (see page 150) is the Berber village of **Setti Fatma** (map E6). Once a quiet rural backwater, Setti Fatma's seven waterfalls have transformed it into a bustling hive of tourism, but if you avoid summer weekends, it's still a charming place in gorgeous surroundings.

Clinging to the side of the mountain, surrounded by snowy peaks and dominated by a rosy pink mosque, the village rests at the very edge of a surging river and in the spring, when the waterfalls are at their most torrential, the place is fragrant with almond blossom.

Reaching the first 10 metre (33ft) -high waterfall is an easy 20 minute walk. On longer hikes to reach the other six, you will need a guide (use an official guide from the **bureau des guides** on the main street). This more strenuous 2–3 hour walk can be made on foot or with a mule, and little side hikes along the river can also be taken. This is the best way to see the countryside in its unspoilt glory, where you will encounter locals tending flocks of sheep, working in their orchards, or washing clothes in the river.

Take your own picnic up here or return to Setti Fatma for lunch, where there are dozens of restaurants on rickety platforms above the water, under the almond trees, clinging to the rocks beside the river, and on rooftops. You'll be hungry after your explorations, so the piping hot tagines, piles of fresh bread, salads, and the obligatory gallons of hot mint tea will be welcome. There is a huge Berber souk here every Monday.

Laze by Lake Lalla-Takerkoust, at the foot of the High Atlas

Just 40km (29 miles) from Marrakech, **Lalla-Takerkoust** (map D7) is a lake created by the French in the 1920s to provide thirsty Marrakech with water and electricity. Over 7km (4 miles) long, this glimmering expanse of turquoise takes the breath away. Days here can be as action-packed or as laid-back as you like.

There are two lovely restaurants on the road that curves round to the right. **Le Flouka** has two pools with views across the lake and a good restaurant on the lake edge, serving typical French fare – *côte de boeuf*, steak tartare – as well as Moroccan specialities.

Next door, **Le Relais du Lac** has a tented camp for overnight stays and a beachy outdoor restaurant serving Moroccan food. They also have a range of activities including quad biking, canoeing, and donkey polo.

On the other side of the lake is a wonderful local restaurant, **Chez Amaghousse**, on a shaded terrace with fantastic views. Lunch is basic (not more than 200dh) but insanely good: grilled chicken, a huge salad, and a plate of chips. They don't serve alcohol, but you can bring your own. From the little beach below the restaurant you can take pedalos out into the lake free of charge.

If after-lunch activities are in order, **Jet Atlas** (www.jet-atlas.com) offers every conceivable watersport: jet-skiing, flyboarding, hover and wake boarding, waterskiing, and even banana boats.

Le Flouka; Barrage Lalla-Takerkoust; tel: 0664 49 26 60; daily L, D; map D7
Le Relais du Lac; Barrage Lalla-Takerkoust; tel: 0524 48 49 43; daily L, D; map D7
Chez Amaghousse; Barrage Lalla-Takerkoust; tel: 0670 01 77 33; map D7

Take to the air on a thrilling helicopter ride

Morocco is a vast country that spans over 400,000 sq kilometres (154,440 sq miles), with the distances between places of interest often entailing several days' travel. The country's natural landscapes are some of the most celebrated and diverse in the world, from towering mountain ranges to surf-battered coastline and from desert to arid steppe. For those visiting Marrakech on a short break, it is impossible to see even a fraction of what this country has to offer. If you want to see Morocco from a compellingly different angle, and in the blink of an eye, what could be more thrilling than a helicopter ride?

The Best of Morocco (www.morocco-travel.com) offers bespoke itineraries involving short helicopter rides of an hour to places like **Kasbah Tamadot** (see page 146) or longer transfers to desert camps in the Sahara. Prices start from £1,700 for an hour in a helicopter seating up to six people. **Voyage to Morocco** (www.voyageto morocco.com) offers several trips ranging from one to five hours and taking in the Atlas, Toubkal region, and palm oases, as well as transfers to **Essaouria** (see page 160) and Merzouga in the Sahara.

Original Travel (www.original travel.co.uk) organises tailored heli-safaris from Marrakech to the desert camp of Dar Ahlam in the Sahara; **Lawrence of Morocco** (www.lawrenceofmorocco. com) offers shorter 30-minute flights over the palm groves of Marrakech. **Dar Azawad** (www.darazawad.com) offers guests helicopter transfers from Marrakech to their exquisite tented camp in the Saharan dunes of the Erg Chigagga.

Go glamping and unwind in the majestic Agafay Desert

Not everyone will have the time to venture into the Sahara, two days from Marrakech, but just 45 minutes away is a desert of such beauty you won't need to. The **Agafay Desert** (map D7) is a breath-taking moonscape stretching to the snow-capped peaks of the Atlas, which rear up to the south.

There are two extraordinary tented camps here, which are out-of-this-world places to visit on a day trip – or, even better, for a night glamping under the stars.

Time seems to stand still at **La Pause**. There is no electricity here so you can appreciate the full effect of the desert sky at night (without light pollution or noise), but the days are beautiful too. Fantastic three-course lunches with wine and soft

drinks are served in huge black Berber tents with uninterrupted views for miles around. There are plenty of activities on hand, too: horse and camel riding, guided hikes, quad and mountain biking, and cooking classes. There is a lovely pool and even a 9-hole golf course in a little canyon edging the property. Accommodation is in luxury tents or stylishly simple pisé lodges.

With 360° views across the desert, **Scarabeo Camp** is a striking bivouac of a dozen white tents, each

Ships of the desert

Riding a camel through the desert is top of many visitors' Moroccan wish-lists; trips can be arranged at both La Pause and Scarabeo Camp. The ride atop these notoriously grumpy animals is actually surprisingly relaxing (although rather bumpy). A vital mode of transport since ancient times, camels are respected throughout Morocco. In some rural areas, people still rely on them to get around, as well as for their milk and meat.

beautifully outfitted with wooden writing desks, cushions, luxurious double beds, Berber carpets, and en-suite showers. At night, the place glows with flickering lanterns and meals are served around a huge communal table. As at La Pause, Scarabeo offers a wealth of things to do, from yoga, massage, and stargazing to off-piste dune-buggy excursions, full-day treks with a picnic, and horse and camel-riding.

It is also possible to arrange a personalised 'Mobile camp' – a smaller version of the main camp erected anywhere of your choosing. Scarabeo will take care of everything from tents and catering to activities, tailor making the glamping holiday of your dreams.

La Pause; Douar Lmih Laroussiene, Commune Agafay; tel: 0610 77 22 40; www.la pause-marrakech.com; daily L, D; map D7
Scarabeo Camp; GPS 31°26.009 N/ 008°12.088W, Commune Agafay; tel: 0662 80 08 23; www.scarabeocamp.com; daily L, D; map D7

Speed through palm groves, countryside, and desert on a quad-biking adventure

If you prefer your holidays to be action packed and adrenalin fuelled, a day of **quad-biking** will be right up your street.

With speeds of up to 130kph (80mph) and a range of exciting terrains – from wild desert to sandy tracks through palm groves, and rough and hilly off-road pistes – you can be as adventurous as you like and you'll see the Moroccan countryside from a thrillingly different perspective.

As well as being able to rent quads for beach rides in Essaouira (see page 160) and in the Agafay Desert (see page 156), there are various companies that offer quad day trips. **DoSomethingDifferent. com** (www.dosomethingdifferent. com) has two tours daily, year-round, at 9am and 2/3pm. For two and a half hours, you will zip through palm groves, desert, and local villages. The tours are led by an experienced driver and include a stop for mint tea and traditional crêpes with honey, as well as hotel transfers. **Dunes & Desert Exploration** (www.dunesdesert. com) has half-day trips that take you across mountains, through wild oases, dry rivers, and a rocky desert, with a stop for tea in a Berber village. Departures are twice daily, at 8.45am and 2.30pm. There is also a full-day excursion that includes a traditional picnic cooked on location, with departures daily at 8.45am. Hotel transfers included. Prices for all start at around 700dh per driver, 350dh per passenger, and 160dh per child. Children under 12 usually restricted.

Behold the highest waterfalls in Morocco

At 110 metres (361ft), the **Cascades d'Ouzoud** are the highest waterfalls in Morocco, plummeting through three major and several minor drops. During the spring (March–June), when the Oued al Abid river runs high, the falls are magnificent; roaring down bright red cliffs into a jade green pool and the canyon far below, which is edged with lime, palm, pomegranate, and olive trees.

Nearby are rickety stalls selling jewellery, pottery, and souvenirs, and some rudimentary cafés serving simple tagines and soft drinks. At the bottom, you get a sense of the full power of the falls with the crash of water and an Evian spray of mist hanging over everything. There are some charming plastic flower-covered wooden barges here that can be hired to paddle about in.

If you want to get away from the touristy throngs around the falls, head to the source (guides can be found in the village), where you can swim in calm pools encircled by exceptional scenery. Unless you decide to take a picnic on this hike, the best place for lunch (also a hotel) is the divinely rustic **Riad Cascades d'Ouzoud**, which has panoramic views over the sur-rounding countryside from its roof terrace and a traditional Berber menu (150dh), with ingredients sourced from local smallholdings. The riad can organise guided treks to the source of the river, the nearby medieval village of Tanermelt, and to the rural souk of Aït Tagla.

The drive to Ouzoud takes around 3 hours.

Riad Cascades d'Ouzoud; Ouzoud; tel: 0662 14 38 04; www.ouzoud.com; map C8

Drive to enchanting Essaouira for a day by the sea

Essaouira (map A8) has been inhabited since Phoenician times, when it produced the famous Tyrean purple dye used on the robes of Roman senators. In the 15th century the Portuguese established it as a free port for Europeans engaged in trans-Saharan gold, ivory, and slave trading. The town itself was built in the 18th century by Alaouite sultan Sidi Mohammed ben Abdallah, who used it as a base for his corsairs.

It first attracted international attention when Orson Welles filmed his *Othello* here and has long been a magnet for artists and travellers. Winston Churchill visited, as did Jimi Hendrix in 1969, and Bob Marley a year later, when the town was a countercultural haven for hippies. Today, it hosts the popular Gnaoua Festival of World Music, the 'Moroccan Woodstock' (www.festival-gnaoua.net). Essaouira's artistic and musical history is still very much the essence of the place, which remains blissfully laid-back. The sleepy medina – a Unesco World Heritage Site – is entirely pedestrian, the souks are a joy to explore, and the beach is a mecca for surfers, windsurfers, and kite surfers.

Place Moulay Hassan is lined with cafés and restaurants: **Café de France** (map B3) is popular; for Italian ice-cream don't miss **Gelateria Dolce Freddo** (map C2). Have a drink on the terrace at **Taros** (tel: 0524 47 64 07; map B3) with its sweeping views across the port. In between the square and the port are the **grilled fish stalls** (*grillades de poissons*; map B2), a great place for a lunch of freshly caught, grilled fish and other seafood.

The main souks are on **Avenue de l'Istiqual** and **Avenue Sidi Mohammed Ben Abdallah**; between Avenue Oqba Ibn Nafi and Place Moulay Hassan you will find an enclave of carpet and kaftan shops. The **ramparts** (*skala*) face the nearby Iles Purpuraires, now the Iles de Mogador, which in the past were used as a quarantine station for pilgrims from

Mecca carrying the plague. Xavier Lecoeur of **Sailing Tour Essaouira** (tel: 0661 62 63 13) runs boat trips around the islands.

Along the **Boulevard Mohammed V** are several fish restaurants, the most popular of which is **La Table by Madada** (7 Rue Youssef el Fassi; tel: 0524 47 55 12; map C2). Unassuming **Triskala** has the best vegan and vegetarian food in town (Rue de Touahen; tel: 0524 47 63 71; map C4), and **Loft Café** (5 Rue Hajjali; tel: 0524 47 63 89; map C3) is another popular place serving fantastic Moroccan-French food in quirky surroundings. At the end of the boulevard are lovely laid-back beach cafés – **Ocean Vagabond** (tel: 0524 78 43 67; map D1) is the best and they also rent surfboards,

Essaouira's artists

Essaouira is popular with artists and around town you will see several fantastic art galleries. The **Damgaard Gallery** (Avenue Oqba Ibn Nafi; map C2) has been exhibiting works by Essaouira's painters since 1988. **Galerie la Kasbah** (4 rue de Tetouan; map C3) is set in an 18th-century riad; there is also **Galerie l'Arbre Bleu** (233 rue Chbanat; map E3) and dozens of others dotted about.

windsurfing and kite surfing equipment, and offer lessons too. Outside Vagabond, horses, camels, and quads can be hired for beach rides. The **Ranch de Diabat** (tel: 0524 47 63 82; map D1) also arranges rides on the beach and into the countryside.

ESSENTIALS

A

ADMISSION CHARGES

Visits to most of Marrakech's monuments and museums are subject to an admission charge. This is normally a small fee of about 10–30dh. If a custodian fulfils an extra service, such as providing a short tour, it is usual to give a tip.

B

BUDGETING

Eating out: A three-course meal for two with Moroccan wine in a mid-range restaurant will cost between 600 and 800dh; a coffee about 10–20dh; and a beer 40–60dh depending on the venue. You can eat in a good but basic restaurant for about 150dh for two without alcohol.

Transport: Hiring a small car for a week from a reputable company costs from around 1,200dh. Hiring a *grand taxi* and driver for the day costs around 1,000dh, depending on distance, often more if organised through your hotel.

C

CHILDREN

Moroccans are very welcoming of children, including in restaurants; however, that may not be the case in some of the foreign-owned riads, so be sure to check that children are welcome when you book. Nappies and formula milk are widely available, usually in grocery shops rather than pharmacies. Some of the larger hotels offer babysitting services.

CLIMATE

The best times to be in Marrakech are late autumn and early spring. Winter is usually bright and sunny, and sometimes warm enough to swim, but it can also be cold, especially at night when temperatures can drop to below freezing. Mid-summer is usually too hot for comfort as temperatures average 33°C (91°F) and top 40°C (104°F).

CLOTHING

In summer pack light cottons; in winter be sure to take both light clothes for daytime and warm clothing (including a coat) for the evening.

Also remember that Morocco is an Islamic country so avoid wearing revealing clothing on the streets. In the evenings, smart-casual is acceptable for most venues. You won't get into some of the more exclusive hotels, like La Mamounia, wearing jeans.

CRIME

Crime is not especially common, but you should take the usual precautions: use a safe in your hotel; don't carry too much cash on you; keep an eye on bags and valuables; and don't leave belongings visible in a parked car. At night be sure to park your car in a guarded car park.

If you are the victim of crime, you will need to report it to the police (there is a Tourist Police station on the north side of the Jemaa el Fna) and obtain an official report to present to your insurer upon your return.

Needless to say, it is inadvisable to buy or use any drugs. There are many Westerners languishing in Moroccan prisons for drug offences.

CUSTOMS AND VISA REQUIREMENTS

The airport Duty Free shop is open to incoming as well as departing passengers. Passengers can import 1 litre of alcohol (wine or spirits); 200 cigarettes or cigarillos or 50 cigars; 150ml of perfume or 250ml of eau de toilette. Up to 2,000dh can be imported. There is no limit on importing foreign currency, though amounts over 100,000dh must be declared. Up to 2,000dh can be exported as well as foreign currencies up to the amount declared on arrival.

Citizens of the UK, Republic of Ireland, US, Canada, Australia, and New Zealand need only a full passport for visits of up to 90 days; the passport must be valid for at least six months after the date you arrive. Visas are not required for stays of less than 90 days. (Visa regulations change, so check before you travel.)

D

DISABLED TRAVELLERS

Disabled access is generally not good in Morocco. High kerbs in the new town and uneven surfaces in the medina make wheelchair use difficult, and most of the museums occupy old palaces or riads with maze-like layouts and lots of steps. Even when restaurants are accessible, the toilets are rarely so. That said, Moroccans are quick to assist where they can.

DRIVING

It is not worth hiring a car for getting around Marrakech, as taxis are so cheap, and many places are inaccessible by car; it is worth it, however, if you want to get out and see the surrounding region. However, if you only want to go to Essaouira you are probably better off getting the Supratours bus or the CTM bus, both of which are cheap and efficient.

Car hire

You can book car hire in advance from home using one of the international companies. However, it is often cheaper to arrange something in situ; most companies have offices in Guéliz. Do try haggling, especially for longer periods. The usual international companies, such as Avis, Hertz, and Europcar, all have local offices and branches in the airport.

The price for a mid-sized car should be 250–300dh per day. Four-wheel drives are around 1,000–1,200dh per day.

Rules of the road

Speed limits are: 40kph (25mph) in urban areas, 100kph (60mph) on the open road, and 120kph (74mph) on motorways (but look out for signs specifying other limits). Be careful to observe these limits: speed-traps are common, especially on approaches to towns. You will receive a small on-the-spot fine for breaking the speed limit.

The old French system of *priorité à droite* (right of way to traffic coming from the right, i.e. vehicles on a roundabout give way to vehicles coming on to it) is being phased out. However, it is still the case on some roundabouts, so approach with care.

As a rule, Moroccans drive quite chaotically but slowly. Dangerous overtaking on main roads is common, so again be cautious.

Petrol tips

Petrol stations are plentiful except on routes through the Atlas, where you should be sure to fill up in advance. Forecourt attendants normally fill the tank for you, and may also clean your windscreen and headlamps (a small tip is welcome but not essential).

Breakdown

Your car hire company should provide you with the number of their breakdown company. Otherwise, flag down a fellow driver and ask for a lift to a repair garage in the nearest town to get assistance.

Parking

Your riad or hotel will be able to advise on parking. If they don't have their own car park, you will need to park in a public car park or on the street. Either way, a *gardien*, who wears an official badge, will keep an eye on your car for a small charge (3–4dh is sufficient for an hour or two, but overnight parking usually costs 15–20dh).

E

ELECTRICITY

The electricity supply is rated 220 volts in all but the very oldest hotels. Plugs are the round two-pin continental type, so bring an adaptor if you want to use UK or US appliances.

EMBASSIES/CONSULATES

Moroccan embassies

UK: 49 Queen's Gate Gardens, London, SW7 5NE; tel: 020-7581 5001; www.moroccanembassylondon.org.uk
US: 1601 21st Street NW, Washington, DC 20009; tel: 202-462 7979; www.embassyofmorocco.us

Moroccan consulate

US: 10 East 40th Street, Floor 23, New York, NY 10016; tel: 212-758 2625; www.moroccanconsulate.com

Embassies in Morocco

British Embassy: 28 Avenue S.A.R Sidi Mohammed, Souissi Rabat 10105; tel: 0537-63 33 33; www.ukinmorocco.fco.gov.uk
British Honorary Consulate: Borj Menara 2, Immeuble B, 5eme etage, Avenue Abdelkrim El Khattabi, Marrakech; tel: 0537 63 33 33
US Embassy: Km 5.7, Avenue Mohammed VI, Souissi Rabat 10170; tel: 0537 63 72 00; www.ma.us embassy.gov

EMERGENCIES

In an emergency, use the following telephone numbers:
Police: **19**

Fire service/ambulance: **15**
The tourist police office is on the north side of the Jemaa el Fna.

ETIQUETTE

In the interests of tourism, Marrakchis are fairly tolerant of the behaviour of foreigners, but it is polite to be respectful of Morocco's Muslim culture and avoid wearing revealing clothes in the medina or indulging in overt displays of physical affection (although holding hands is fine). During Ramadan try to avoid eating, drinking and smoking on the streets in daylight hours.

Non-Muslims cannot enter working mosques in Morocco.

F

FESTIVALS

The festival calendar is getting busier year on year, as new festivals are added to boost year-round interest in the city. Some of the main ones are:

January: Marrakech Marathon; www.marathon-marrakech.com
February: Marrakech Biennale – city-wide contemporary arts festival held every two years; www.marrakech biennale.org
April: Marathon des Sables – the most gruelling footrace on earth; www.marathondessables.co.uk
FIA WTCC Race of Morocco – Marrakech's Grand Prix; www.marrakech grandprix.com
June/July: Essaouira's Gnaoua World Music Festival takes over the town; www.festival-gnaoua.net

July: The Festival National des Arts Populaires de Marrakech takes place at El Badi Palace, celebrating local folklore
September: The Oasis Music Festival – house and electro music festival in the foothills of the Atlas; www.the oasisfest.com
October: TEDxMarrakech – international forum, now in its 6th year in Marrakech; www.tedxmarrakesh.net
December: Marrakech International Film Festival – held in early December in the Palais des Congrès, the Théâtre Royal, and various smaller venues. A giant screen is erected on the Jemaa el Fna's western side; www.festival marrakech.info.

H

HEALTH

No vaccinations are required for entry into Morocco unless you have come from a yellow fever, cholera, or small pox zone.

Morocco has good doctors and most pharmacies have a good supply of drugs. If you need to see a doctor or dentist during your stay in Morocco, staff in your hotel/riad will be able to help you in finding one.

The best hospital is the **Clinique Internationale de Marrakech**; Route de l'aeroport, Bab Ighli; tel: 0524 36 95 95.

Insurance

All medical care must be paid for so be sure to take out adequate health insurance before you travel.

Stomach upsets

These are easily avoided if a few simple precautions are taken: don't eat food that has been left standing or reheated (food stalls should not be a problem as the food is cooked to order), peel fruit, treat salads with circumspection, and only drink bottled water. If you are struck down, drink plenty of water, preferably with rehydration salts, and take a diarrhoea remedy (available at pharmacies).

A local remedy for upset stomachs is cactus fruit, also known as Barbary fig, sold from stands on street corners. For a few dirhams the vendor will peel one or two for you while you wait.

HOURS AND HOLIDAYS

Business hours

Shops in the medina: Sat–Thu 10am–8pm, some also open Fri.
Shops in Guéliz: Mon–Sat 10am–1.30pm and 3.30–7.30pm, closed Sun.
Banks: Winter: Mon–Fri 8.30–11.30am and 2.30–4pm; summer: Mon–Fri 8.30–11.30am and 3–5pm; Ramadan: Mon–Fri 9.30am–3pm.
All hours are variable, subject to change, and dependent on the vendor.

State holidays

New Year's Day: 1 Jan
Independence Manifesto Day: 11 Jan
Labour Day: 1 May
Feast of the Throne: 30 July

Reunification Day: 14 Aug
People's Revolution Day: 20 Aug
Youth Day and birthday of King Mohammed VI: 21 Aug
Anniversary of Green March: 6 Nov
Independence Day: 18 Nov

Muslim holidays

These are governed by the Hegira lunar calendar and are, therefore, movable. The holidays get earlier by 11 days each year (12 in a leap year). Exact dates depend on the sighting of the new moon.
Mouloud: The Prophet's birthday
Aid es Seghir (marking the end of Ramadan)
Aid el Kebir (feast of Abraham's sacrifice of a lamb instead of his son)
Muslim New Year

I

INTERNET

There are numerous internet cafés and some of the *téléboutiques* also offer internet access. The Cyber Parc at the foot of Avenue Mohammed V has internet booths scattered around the park as well as an indoor internet station. Internet access costs from 10dh an hour; many of the better hotels offer Wi-Fi.

L

LANGUAGE

Moroccans speak their own dialect of Arabic, but written communication is in classical Arabic. There are also various Berber dialects, and in the Marrakech region it is *chleuh*. Although most Berbers understand Arabic, few Arabs understand Berber.

French is also widely spoken and understood, although fluency is not as widespread as it used to be, partly because children are no longer taught in French in state schools.

Useful phrases in Arabic

Hello *salaam aleikum*
Welcome *Ahlan wa sahlan*
Good morning *Sbah l-khir*
Good evening *Msa l-khir*
Goodbye *Beslama/masalama*
How are you? *La bes?*
I'm fine *labes*
Please *'Afak*
Thank you *Shukran*
Yes/No *Iyyeh/Lla*
What's your name? *Ashnu smitek?*
My name is... *Smiti...*
Where are you from? *Mnin nta? (to a man); mnin nti?* (to a woman)
I'm from England/the US *Ana men inglatirra/amrika*
Do you speak English/French? *Wash kat-kellem l-ingliziya/l-fransawiya?*
I don't understand *Ma f-hemt-sh*
What does this mean? *Ashnu kat'ni hadi?* (for feminine); *Ashnu kay'ni hada?* (for masculine)
Never mind *Ma'alish*
It's forbidden *Mamnu'*
What time is it? *Shal f sa'a?*

Emergencies

I need help *Bghit musa'ada*
Hospital *Sbitar*
Pharmacy *Farmasyan*
Diarrhoea *S-haal*
Police *Bolis*

Getting around

Where? *Feen?*
Downtown *Wust l-mdina*
Taxi *Taxi*
Grand/shared taxi *Taxi kbir*
Aeroplane *Tiyyara*
Station *Mahatta, la station*
To/From *Al/Men*
Right/Left *Limen/Lsser*

LGBTQ TRAVEL

Homosexuality is, in theory, illegal, and can incur a prison sentence of three months to three years. It is, therefore, important to approach gay encounters with Moroccans with caution; it could be a set-up or there may be an economic motive. That said, Marrakech has long been a centre for expatriate male homosexuality, and many foreign-owned riads offer discreet places to stay.

M

MAPS

A free and up-to-date map is distributed by the tourist office but its coverage of the souk area is sketchy.

In addition to the maps found in this book, the best available maps are *Insight FlexiMap Marrakech*, published by Apa Publications; *Marrakech & Essaouira* published by Editions Laure Kane; and Michelin map no. 742, which covers the whole of Morocco and features a useful enlargement of Marrakech.

MEDIA

Publications

There is a range of daily and weekly publications in French and Arabic. The two main publications in French are the pro-Royal *Le Matin* and the more liberal *L'Opinion*. Weeklies include the outspoken *TelQuel*. *Le Monde* is also widely available, as are some English newspapers, but the latter will be at least a day old by the time you buy them. For listings of forthcoming events consult the monthly *Tribune de Marrakech*, *Couleurs Maroc*, and *Marrakech Mag*, available in hotel and restaurant foyers and kiosks.

Television

Most hotels provide CNN and BBC World satellite channels. Morocco has two state-run TV channels, 2M and TVM, which are more interesting than they used to be, providing that you can understand French or Arabic, but far from essential viewing. It also operates two privately run satellite channels, Al Maghribiya and Mid 1 Sat.

MONEY

The Moroccan currency is the dirham (dh). The dirham is a reasonably stable currency. Recent exchange rates have hovered around 12dh to £1 sterling, 11dh to €1, and 10dh to $1. Rates vary between banks, so shop around.

ATMs

ATMs are the easiest way of obtaining cash, although your bank may charge you a handling fee as well as interest if you are using a credit card (you can often use debit cards bearing the Cirrus logo, but don't rely on this alone). ATMs are plentiful in the Ville Nouvelle and there are a couple of Banque Populaire ATMs at the top of Rue Bab Agnaou, off the Jemaa el Fna. The daily limit on withdrawals is currently 2,000dh (though different banks may allow up to 4,000dh).

Credit cards

MasterCard and Visa are accepted in most hotels, petrol stations, and the more expensive shops and restaurants. Other cards are less widely accepted.

P

POLICE

Most matters concerning tourists are handled by the tourist police, who have a station on the northern side of the Jemaa el Fna (tel: 0524 38 45 01).

POST

The main post office (PTT) is on Place 16 Novembre in Guéliz. Stamps are available from tobacconists.

R

RELIGION

Islam

Morocco is a comparatively tolerant Muslim country, but religion is still the biggest influence on society. The five requirements of Islam –

affirmation that there is no other god but God and Mohammed is his Prophet; prayer five times a day (you will hear the call to prayer throughout the city); the observance of Ramadan; the giving of alms to the poor; and making the *hadj* (pilgrimage) to Mecca at least once in a lifetime – are central to many Moroccan lives.

Officially, Morocco follows the Sunni (orthodox) branch of Islam. However, there are many thriving Sufi brotherhoods that promote a more mystical approach to God.

Ramadan

The Muslim month of fasting has some disadvantages for travellers. Restaurants and cafés are much quieter during the day (some even close for the month) and some restaurants that normally sell alcohol do not during this time. It is impolite to eat or drink in public during Ramadan.

Christianity

Marrakech has a small Christian community, served by the little Catholic church in Guéliz (see page 115).

T

TELEPHONES

Phone booths are plentiful. They are operated with phone cards sold at tobacconists. In addition you will find *téléboutiques* where you can use coins and get change from the attendant.

To make an international call, dial 00 for an international line, followed by the country code (44 for the UK). Remember to drop the initial zero of the UK area code you are dialling.

Mobile phones

To use your own mobile phone in Morocco you should check costs with your own mobile phone company before leaving home. Alternatively, you can buy a prepaid mobile phone while in Morocco or a SIM card for use in your own phone. These are available from Maroc Telecom, Inwi, or Meditel, which have numerous outlets.

TIME

Morocco keeps to Greenwich Mean Time all year round.

TIPPING

It is usual to tip porters, chambermaids, other hotel staff if they are particularly helpful, and waiting staff. There are no hard-and-fast rules for the amount: 10 percent would be considered generous.

TOURIST INFORMATION

The main tourist office is on Place Abdel Moumen Ben Ali in Guéliz (tel: 0524 43 61 79). It is open Mon–Fri 8.30am–noon and 2.30–6.30pm, Sat 9am–noon and 3–6pm.

TOURS

There are countless local companies offering a wide range of tours, from short guided tours in Marrakech to excursions into the

Atlas and southern Morocco. Two reputable companies are: **Ribat Tours** (Passage Prince Moulay Rachid, Guéliz; tel: 0524 42 98 98; www.ribatours.com), which specialises in outdoor activities, and **Terres et Voyages** (Immeuble D1, 8 Avenue 11 Janvier, Bab Doukkala; tel: 0524 43 71 53; www.terreset voyages.com), a reliable mainstream tour operator, that has an English-speaking owner.

TRANSPORT

Arrival by air

Royal Air Maroc operates a daily flight to Marrakech from London Heathrow and Gatwick via Casablanca. Sometimes this involves a long delay in Casablanca while waiting for connecting flights from other countries in Europe.

Royal Air Maroc in the UK: Langham House, 32–33 Gosfield Street, London W1W 6ED; tel: 020-7307 5840; www.royalairmaroc.com.

Royal Air Maroc in Marrakech: 197 Avenue Mohammed V; tel: 0524 42 55 03; www.royalairmaroc.com.

Marrakech is well served by the following budget airlines:

Easyjet (www.easyjet.com), which flies from Gatwick.

Ryanair (www.ryanair.com), which flies from London Luton and London Stansted.

Thomsonfly (www.thomsonfly.com), which flies from Manchester, London Gatwick, and Birmingham.

British Airways (www.ba.com), which flies from London Gatwick.

Airport

Upon arrival you will be required to fill out an immigration form before going through passport control. The arrivals hall has the usual facilities, including a bank and cash machine, and car hire firms. There are three terminals.

On departure you will also need to fill out an immigration form before passing through passport control. The café in the departure lounge will take euros as well as dirhams.

From the Airport. Marrakech-Menara Airport is situated 6km (4 miles) from the city centre. There is normally a plentiful supply of taxis outside the terminal. The fare into town should be no more than 100dh, although you will probably be asked for about 200dh in the first instance so be prepared to bargain. There is a board showing what the rates should be outside the terminal. Some drivers will accept euros if you do not have dirhams. There is also an irregular bus service (no. 11) to the Jemaa el Fna every 30 minutes or so.

Transport within Marrakech

Taxis. There are two types of taxi in Morocco: *petits taxis* (greeny-beige livery) and *grands taxis* (large cream Mercedes).

Petits taxis take up to three passengers and can be hired on the street. Fares are very cheap, but the meter is often broken so you must negotiate a set price before you get in the car. It is not unusual for people to share *petits taxis*, so don't be surprised if your driver picks up another passenger or two along the way.

Grands taxis take up to six passengers. You can charter a *grand taxi* for the day or for a longer trip (easily arranged through your hotel, or more cheaply by negotiating directly with drivers at the *grands-taxis* stations). In Guéliz the main station is next door to the train station on Avenue Hassan II.

City buses. There is a good bus service, although buses can get very crowded. One of the most useful buses for tourists is the no. 1 from Place de Foucauld to Place Abdel Moumen Ben Ali. Other useful routes are nos 2 and 10 for the bus station, and nos 3 and 8 for the train station. The flat fare on all buses is 3.5dh. Payment is made upon boarding; drivers will supply change for smaller notes. www.alsa.ma has bus routes and tariffs.

Calèches. Horse-drawn carriages congregate outside the larger hotels and at various points around the city, most notably opposite Club Med on Place de Foucauld. Official prices are posted inside the *calèche* but be sure to check the price with the driver before boarding (see page 38).

Trains. The entrance to Marrakech's train station is on Avenue Mohammed VI. The station runs direct services to Casablanca, Rabat, Fez, Tangier, and Meknès. For information: tel: 0524 44 77 23; www.oncf.ma.

Long-distance bus/coach travel. Supratours (Avenue Hassan II, Gare ONCF & bab Doukkala; tel: 0524 42 17 69; www.supratours.ma) and CTM (12 Boulevard Zerktouni, Gueliz; tel: 0800 0900 30; www.ctm.ma) are the most useful companies and both have Wi-fi on their buses.

V

VISAS AND PASSPORTS

Holders of full British passports or American passports can enter Morocco for a stay of up to three months without a visa, but their passport must be valid for at least six months after the planned departure date.

W

WEBSITES

National Tourist Office (in English): www.visitmorocco.com
Official hotel booking and travel tips: www.morocco.com
Good list of riads and restaurant guide: www.hipmarrakech.com
Events, hotel, and restaurant listings: www.madeinmarrakech.com
Bespoke luxury holidays across Morocco: www.lawrenceofmorocco.com
Restaurant listings: www.best restaurantsmaroc.com

WOMEN TRAVELLERS

Women travellers do occasionally receive a low level of harassment, but this usually remains a mild irritant rather than anything more threatening. Keep hassle to a minimum by behaving coolly but courteously, wearing modest clothing and avoiding eye contact.

INDEX

A

admission charges 162
Agafey Desert 156
Agdal Gardens 26, 19
airport 170
air transport 170
Amelkis Golf Resort 21
argan oil 44, 63
art galleries 93, 118
Asni 146
Atlas Marrakech Tennis Academy 21
Atlas Mountains 19, 24
Avenue de l'Istiqual (Essaouira) 160
Avenue Sidi Mohammed Ben Abdallah (Essaouira) 160

B

Bab Agnaou 38
Bab Ahmar 38
Bab Dbagh 38
Bab Doukkala 87
Bab el Khemis 38
Bab Ghmat 38
Badi Palace 17, 36, 60, 68
Bahia Palace 17
Beldi (spa-hammam and hotel) 130
Ben Youssef Madrassa 17
Bert Flint Museum at Maison Tiskiwin 79
Boulevard Mohammed V (Essaouira) 161
budgeting 162
buses 171
business hours 166

C

calèches (horse-drawn carriages) 38, 171
car breakdown 164
car hire 163
carpets 52
Cascades d'Ouzoud 24
cemeteries 19, 71
Central Medina 26, 34
childcare 162
Chrob ou Chouf Fountain 17, 87
climate 162
clothing 162
coaches 171
consulates 164
cookery classes 90
credit cards 168
crime 162
customs and visa requirements 163

D

Dar Bellarj 99
Dar Cherifa 45
Dar el Bacha 93
Dar Si Said Museum (Museum of Moroccan Arts) 23
desert adventures 155, 156, 158
disabled travellers 163
driving 163

E

EcoMusée Berbère 89, 151
Eid (religious festival) 71
electricity 164
embassies/consulates 164
emergencies 164
Essaouira 25, 27
Essaouria 155
essentials 168
etiquette 165

European cemetery 19

F

festivals 165
fondouks (merchants' workshops) 98
fortune-telling 11

G

gay travellers 165
golf 136
Guéliz 9, 23

H

haggling tips 40
Hammam Dar el Bacha 12, 101
Hammam de la Rose 13
health 165
helicopter rides 24
High Atlas Mountains 24, 25
horse-drawn carriages (calèches) 38, 171
hot-air ballooning 21
hotels
    Auberge Sanglier Qui Fume 148
    Bab Hotel 18
    Beldi Country Club 130
    Chez Juju 149
    Dar Azawad 155
    Dar Cherifa 45
    Four Seasons 133
    Hotel Islane 36
    Hotel La Renaissance 113
    Jardins de la Koutoubia 15
    Jnane Tamsna 135
    Kasbah Bab Ourika 151
    Kasbah du Toubkal 146

Kasbah Tamadot 146, 155
Ksar Char-Bagh 133
La Maison Arabe 91
La Mamounia 15, 26
La Roseraie 148
Le Bled 130
Le Bled de Grenadine 130
Le Relais du Lac 154
Les Deux Tours 130
Les Jardins de la Medina 15, 48
L'Oliveraie de Marigha 148
Peacock Pavilions 135
Riad 74
Riad Cascades d'Ouzoud 159
Riad el Fenn 15
Royal Mansour 51
Samanah Country Club 137
hours and holidays 166

I

Imlil 146
internet 166

J

Jardin Majorelle 19, 27
Jbel Toubkal 146
Jebel Oukaimeden 149
Jemaa el Fna 10, 11
Jewish cemetery 19
Jewish Quarter (mellah) 26, 67, 71

K

kaftans 61
Koubba el Badiyin 17
Koutoubia Gardens 36
Koutoubia Mosque and Minaret 17, 26
Ksar Char-Bagh 13

L

Lalla-Takerkoust 25, 27

La Maison Arabe 90
language 167
La Safranière 150
Lazama Synagogue 71
Les Bains de Marrakech (spa-hammam) 13

M

Madrassa Ben Youssef 26
Maison de la Photographie 23
Maison Tiskiwin (Bert Flint Museum) 23
maps 40
Marrakech Biennale 118
Marrakech Region 27
media 168
medical insurance 166
medina walls 38
Menara Gardens and Pavilion 19, 27
mint tea 88
money 168
Mouassine Fountain 102
Musée de l'Art de Vivre 99
Musée de Marrakech 17, 40, 86
Museum of Moroccan Arts (Dar Si Said) 74

N

nightlife
African Chic 18
Bo et Zin 128
Grand Casino La Mamounia 72
Jad Mahal 18, 117
Kechmara 18
Le Comptoir 14
Le Comptoir Darna 128
Le Palace 128
Lotus 117
Montecristo 117
Renaissance Bar 113
Sky Bar 113

So Bar 117
SO Lounge 128
Suite Club 128
Theatro 18
Nikki Beach 130
Northern Medina 26, 84

O

Ouirgane 148
Oukaimeden 149
Ourika Valley 24

P

Palmeraie Palace 20
pampering 13
parking 164
passports 171
petrol 164
Place Ben Youssef 86
Place des Ferblantiers 60
Place Moulay Hassan (Essaouira) 160
police 168
post 168

Q

quad-biking 158

R

ramparts (Essaouira) 160
ramparts (Marrakech) 17
Ranch de Diabat (horse riding Essaouira) 161
religion 168
restaurants and cafés
Auberge Au Sanglier qui Fume 148
Café Arabe 46
Café Clock 69
Café de France (Essaouira) 160
Café des Epices 39
Chez Amaghousse 154
Chez Bejgueni 86, 10
Chez Chegrouni 35
Dar Moha 49

Dar Yacout 14
Dar Zellij 14
Gelateria Dolce Freddo (Essaouira) 160
Grand Café de la Poste 114
Jad Mahal 14
Kaowa 109
Katsura 120
Kosybar 60, 62
La Grande Table Marocaine 51
La Roseraie 24
La Terrasse des Epices 46
Le Bagatelle 112
Le 16 Café 122
Le Flouka 154
Le Fondouk 14
Le Français 72
Le Marocain 72
Le Marrakchi 35
Le Pavillon de la Piscine 73
Le Tanjia 60, 62
Le Tobsil 49
L'Italien 72
L'Oliveraie de Marigha 148
Méchoui Alley 10
Ocean Vagabond (Essaouira) 161
Souk Café 102
Taros (Essaouira) 160
Un Déjeuner à Marrakech 75
Riad Denise Masson 99
road rules 163
Royal Golf de Marrakech 20
Royal Tennis Club 132
rue Amsefah 98
rue Dar el Bacha 87, 93
Rue Riad Zitoun el Jdid 75
rue Souk Ahl Fes 98

S

Saadian Tombs 17
Sahara Desert 156
Samanah Country Club 21
Setti Fatma 24
shopping
    Akbar Delights 43
    Aladdin's caves 94
    Al-Kawtar 44
    Al-Kawtar (bed- and table-linen etc.) 44
    Assouss Cooperative d'Argan (cosmetics) 44
    Assouss Cooperative d'Argan (salad oils) 44
    Atelier Moro 43
    Atika 111
    Au Fil d'Or 43
    Aya's 61
    Beldi 43
    Ben Rahal 53
    Coopérative Artisanale des Femmes de Marrakech 44
    Côté Sud 110
    Criée Berbère (carpet auctions) 8
    Darkoum 110
    David Bloch Gallery 119
    El Louami Ahmed 75
    Ensemble Artisanal 50
    Galerie 118
    Galerie d'Art Lawrence Arnott 119
    Galerie des Tanneurs 111
    Galerie Noir sur Blanc 119
    Galerie Ré 118
    Galerie Tindouf 118
    Grande Bijouterie 9, 78
    Heritage Berber 109
    Intensité Nomade 111
    Jamade 75
    Jemaa el Fna 10, 11
    Kaftan Queen 61, 111
    Kamal 47
    Khalid Art Gallery 93
    Kulchi 43
    La Cotonnière 111
    La Criée Berbère (carpet auctions) 39, 52
    La Maison de Bahira 47
    La Maison de l'Artisanat 94
    Les Maîtres du Pain 122
    Librarie Dar el Bacha 93
    L'Orientaliste 110
    Matisse Art Gallery 118
    Mellah Market 8, 67
    Mergen Alaoui 47
    Michèle Baconnier 61, 111
    Ministero del Gusto 23
    Mustafa No.1's 37
    Mustapha Blaoui 94
    Nectarome 150
    Original Marrakech 47
    Place Vendôme 111
    Rue Dar el Bacha 9, 93
    Souk Cherratin (leather goods) 40
    Souk Chouari (carpenters blacksmiths) 41
    Souk des Bijoutiers (jewellery) 41
    Souk des Teinturiers (dyers textiles) 41
    Souk el Attarine (spices metalware) 40
    Souk el Kebir (leather goods) 40
    Souk el Khemis (flea market) 9, 26, 38, 87, 95

Souk Haddadine (carpenters blacksmiths) 41
Souk Kimakhine (musical instruments) 41
Souk Sebbaghine (dyers textiles) 41
Souk Semmarine (textiles kaftans pashminas) 40
Souk Smata (slippers) 40
Spice Square (Rahba Kedima) 8, 22, 39
Warda la Mouche 75

Zimroda 93
skiing 149
Southern Medina 26, 61
spas 48, 51, 66, 101, 133
sport 20, 136
street food 10, 37
swimming pools 48

T

Tafza 151
taxis 170
tea ritual 88
telephones 169
time 169
tipping 169
Tnine Ourika 150

Tour des Ramparts 38
tourist information 169
tours 169
trains 171
transport 170

V

visas 171

W

websites 171
women travellers 171

Z

Zaouia Sidi Bel Abbes 87, 97